THE OFFSITE

The Offsite

A *LEADERSHIP CHALLENGE* FABLE

Robert H. Thompson

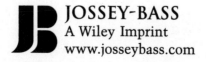

JOSSEY-BASS
A Wiley Imprint
www.josseybass.com

Published by Jossey-Bass
A Wiley Imprint
989 Market Street, San Francisco, CA 94103-1741—www.josseybass.com

Library of Congress Cataloging-in-Publication Data
Thompson, Robert H.
    The offsite : a *leadership challenge* fable / Robert H. Thompson.—1st ed.
    p. cm.
    ISBN 978-0-470-18982-5 (cloth)
    1. Leadership. I. Title.
  HD57.7.T4674 2008
  658.4'092—dc22
                                                    2007041310

Printed in the United States of America
FIRST EDITION
HB Printing 10 9 8 7 6 5 4 3 2 1

CONTENTS

Foreword

I was talking with an author friend of mine a while back about the challenges of writing fiction. As someone who exclusively writes nonfiction, I am in awe of people with the talent to create characters, imagine things that have never happened, and craft lines of dialogue. My friend shared the same apprehensions and amazement, and he related a conversation with an author who writes mostly novels.

It seems that in writing one particular scene in a detective novel, a lead character entered an apartment building late at night, walked up the long, narrow staircase, and knocked on the door at the top of the landing. The door opened, and a barely visible figure from inside the apartment pulled a gun and shot the man. He tumbled down the stairs, stone cold dead. Said the novelist about this development, "I was in a real predicament. I needed that guy in the next chapter!"

I love that story. It illustrates how fiction takes on a life of its own. How it shifts and changes as each character develops, as each scene progresses, as each interaction plays out. And that's exactly what Robert Thompson relates in his introduction to *The Offsite*. His characters took on lives of their own. They'd wake him up at night, talk to him, nag him, argue with him, praise him, encourage him, elude him, be uncooperative, change course, surprise him, but in the end offer him a unique way of viewing the world. That's what makes this book so special. Robert has offered us all, through his characters, the opportunity to examine The Five Practices of Exemplary Leadership®—the model that Barry Posner and I developed nearly 25 years ago in the first edition of *The Leadership Challenge*—in a unique and playful way that gives new life and meaning to what leaders do when they are functioning at their best.

In *The Offsite* you'll meet Abby, Charlie, Gwen, Jerry, Sam, Joe, and Gordon. I think you'll recognize them as folks you've met at an offsite you attended. I know I did. Like all memorable characters in a well-told tale, they each have their own quirks and redeeming qualities. They each have their own personal back-stories. They will sometimes amuse you, sometimes annoy you, and sometimes enlighten you. But most of all, they will teach you, each through a personal realization or two. And that is the power of a good story. A good story teaches, and this does that with every turn of the page.

One of my favorite works of fiction is *The Prime of Miss Jean Brodie*. In the film adaptation of Muriel Spark's classic, there's a scene during which Headmistress MacKay calls Miss Brodie to her office to chastise Miss Brodie for her somewhat unorthodox teaching methods. Headmistress MacKay comments on the precocity of Miss Brodie's students. Miss Brodie accepts this as a compliment, not a criticism, and says:

"To me education is a leading out. The word education comes from the root 'ex,' meaning 'out,' and 'duco,' 'I lead.' To me education is simply a leading out of what is already there."

To this Headmistress MacKay responds rather haughtily, saying, "I had hoped there might also be a certain amount of putting in."

Miss Brodie laughs at this notion and replies, "That would not be education, but intrusion."

We agree. The process of personal development should never be intrusive. It should never be about just filling someone full of facts or skills. It won't work. Education should always be liberating. It should be about releasing what is already inside.

The quest for leadership is first an inner quest to discover who you are.

So, sit back, turn the page, and begin a journey of self-discovery along with the characters in this finely crafted book.

Orinda, California   Jim Kouzes
November 2007

Introduction

"Wake up, get some paper and a pen . . . I have something to share." That's what startled me as I awoke from a deep sleep one night. No, I wasn't hallucinating. Charlie, a key story character, had started to talk to me. Then other characters chimed in from time to time, filling in who they were and what they should do. That's when the concept of the book you are holding started to jell.

Family, friends, and colleagues have been after me to "write the book" for years. There were many false starts. The first iteration was aimed at creating another "leadership researched" approach. Since I happen to be associated with two of the best leadership researchers, I jettisoned that method early. Then I tried the "I am a trained reporter" tactic and busily interviewed clients and others in yet another ill-conceived effort. I also attempted the "I have this workbook that could be turned into a book" approach. Once again, dull as dishwater.

Once all the characters became a chorus in my head and in my home, it was "game on." Family members began to use them to talk to me as well. "Dad, Charlie should do this," was the refrain at many dinners.

So armed with stories from numerous workshops, coaching interactions, and personal experience, the characters' nonstop nudging assisted in creating the final context and helped pierce through my stubborn gray matter to unearth the insights that make up this book.

A key thought is that leadership is not about position. It's a personal choice that creates a new way of being. The potential resides at our core, only revealed by a spark of passion. Passion and leadership are intertwined. Never satisfied, leaders have a strong desire to change things . . . from the PTA to the USA to the world. In their life work, they create a legacy for themselves and others. They create their masterpiece.

Early in my career, I paid scant attention to this leadership stuff. I just did what I was told while dreaming about making others do as I said. Decades later, much to my surprise, I found myself teaching it. I taught and I learned.

One important lesson became clear. If your passion has ebbed or your commitment to leadership is waning, there is good news. You are never too old or too young to shift your behaviors. In the words of Jim Kouzes and Barry Posner, who have generously welcomed this book into their *Leadership Challenge* fold, "Leadership is for everyone." It's your choice.

I hope the story that ultimately emerged sparks your passion. And one day you can look back on your life and be proud of your own masterpiece.

Join us. Meet the characters. They are all amalgams of my sleepy imagination blended with real-life people I've encountered over the years. The setting is a hotel in Tucson, Arizona. Folks are flying in for that sometimes-agonizing mini-vacation . . . the company offsite. Enjoy!

THE OFFSITE

PART ONE

Arrivals

CHAPTER 1

The Revolution Begins
Monday–12:07 PM
(Tucson, Arizona)

"It's been quite a while, Ms. Bancroft," said the dark-haired woman with a smile. "Welcome to La Mariposa Resort & Spa."

Abby glanced up from the usual check-in paperwork, drawn to the warmth in the woman's voice. "Thanks," she said. "Do I know you?" She was terrible with names. She blamed it on all the travel—the constant coming and going; it took the individual aspects of people and places and blurred them together into one continuous watered-down scene like the paintings hanging over beds in chain hotels. But the woman was still smiling and there was something familiar about her face.

"Mary Mitchell. We met a few years ago," the woman said, reaching out to shake Abby's hand. "Your seminar here—it changed my life."

A fellow revolutionary, thought Abby with a grin. *I'm glad to hear it.* "What group were you with?" she asked, flipping through the sessions in her mind, searching for this face among the crowded rooms.

"I wasn't with a group, Ms. Bancroft, I was your . . . uh . . . waitress. Seems like yesterday. It was a difficult time in my life, I was a single mom and in serious financial trouble." Her voice trailed off and Abby could see emotion in her eyes as she recounted her story.

"I remember the day my manager told me you wanted to see me in the conference room you had booked for the sessions. I was very worried because I thought I'd done something wrong. I arrived in the room and you made me stand beside you in front of the whole group. I could feel my face turn red with embarrassment. Then you asked the entire room to thank me for my work during your conference. What you did for me, the applause, it made me feel like somebody important, like I mattered," said Mary. "It really turned things around for me."

"Suddenly, my job and I mattered again. I'm sure those Five Practices I overheard you speak of made the difference. I decided to go back to school to train in hotel management. I was fortunate enough to earn the assistant manager position here at La Mariposa. When I saw your name on the conference schedule, I knew I had to thank you."

"Mary, that's great," said Abby, shaking her head. It never ceased to amaze her, the changes people could undergo when they really got it. "Would you and your staff join us later this week for some more applause and embarrassment?"

"That would be really great . . . sure. I'm always telling my staff about you. I have a great group, they will serve you well. I look forward to seeing their shocked faces," chuckled Mary.

Abby glanced toward the double doors and the waiting bellman. "I've got to get settled but I'll be in touch."

Abby loved this place. The warm caress of desert breezes, the sun shimmering off the Santa Catalina Mountains. In all her years of coaching and speaking, this was one of her favorite off-site locations. And she was excited at the thought of being able to get together with Sam Arthur, her mentor and now primary investor in her new business effort, Perfect Leadership Consulting. His expertise and deep research into leadership, plus his investment, had been the key to her success. And he was always so modest about his achievements. Lately, he'd said he was dabbling in the hotel business. She was not sure what that meant, but she knew it would be interesting to find out.

As she made her way across the grounds, she shifted her thoughts to the week ahead. Her mission was to help two pharmaceutical companies build a cohesive team for the product sales joint venture they were trying to put together. Charlie Verona, the key facilitator, would be put to the test. His group had a real pistol of a problem in it, a sales veep named Joe Vanderson. They'd have to put their heads together on that guy before the first session. She looked forward to seeing Charlie again, not only to put a plan of action together on how to combat the potential Joe problem, but also to share his company. Being on the road for so long made her crave some familiarity. And Charlie always seemed to bring out the cravings, in spite of the fact she had Dennis patiently waiting at home for her . . . waiting for an answer she just wasn't ready to give him yet.

CHAPTER 2

I'm Perfect; You're Perfect

Monday—12:14 PM

Gwen Kelly shuffled through the files in her lap. *This is it,* she thought, pulling her speech out of its well-worn folder. The usual rah rah. *I should've been a cheerleader. Go Sales! If only that would work.* She hit the flight attendant call button and ordered another club soda. The three-hour flight from San Jose through Phoenix to Tucson gave her too much time to think. Sales were down, the market had shifted, and there wasn't much coming through the pipeline in terms of new products. Her two years at Advanced Biomolecular Pharmaceuticals had been rocky, to say the least. *But it's not all market related,* Gwen thought, slumping back in her seat. *My team is falling apart.*

When Jerry Allen, the new vice president for business development, first announced the partnership meeting in

Tucson, Gwen had thought her speech would write itself. Now it held the allure of wallpaper paste; thin, watery, unlikely to stick. *We just need to work the numbers,* muttered Gwen, staring out the window as the flight began its descent into Tucson. *Beat the bushes. Solve the problem. Motivate the team. If we don't pull it together this week, I'm going to need that interview with Eastridge Executive Recruitment.*

The idea to engage a headhunter had actually been her husband's. He was always extremely supportive of her and had a way of zeroing in on her doubts and still make her feel like a superstar. "Whatever makes you happy," he would tell her.

She'd sat on the idea for a few months, but when things at ABP deteriorated, she'd called Eastridge.

"Welcome to La Mariposa," said the attendant as her shuttle door opened. "May I take your bags?"

Gwen entered the lobby and headed for the registration desk. *Perfect,* she thought, taking in the hotel's rich décor. *I could get used to this.* She wished her husband were here to see it and share it too. His phrase of affirmation was still ringing in her ears: "Whatever makes you happy."

Happy. *What would make me happy?* Gwen wondered, gazing out her second-story window. Happiness would be one of those *Star Trek* devices letting you flit about the galaxy on business and still make it home in time for baths and bedtime stories.

Looking out over the pool, she saw a silver-haired gardener washing the deck with a decisive spray of his hose. She could almost hear him singing. No worries at all. She sighed. *Gardening, now that's a thought. I could chuck it all and plant flowers. I bet no one thinks he's too controlling.*

The thought chafed against her already bruised ego as she remembered her last performance review. That's what it said. *But how am I supposed to get them to do what needs to be done if I don't control the situation?* She knew her head was on the chopping block and Jerry was holding the axe. If this meeting didn't produce some results, Gwen knew where the axe would fall. Jerry was a piece of the puzzle that Gwen hadn't quite placed. Was it her performance or something else rubbing him raw?

She thought back a month to a scene in the office. "Hey boss," said Gwen, leaning against Jerry's doorframe. It was Friday afternoon. "You got a few minutes? I'm at my wit's end."

Jerry, somewhat startled, looked up. He ran his fingers through his prematurely graying hair as if to erase a thought. He'd been hoping for a bit more quiet time, but the look on Gwen's face had him shuffling his schedule at least a half-hour back.

"First things first—don't call me boss," he said with a half-smile as he filed some papers back in his inbox. "It reminds me of the mob, and it has a negative, subservient ring to it, don't ya think? What's on your mind?"

"I just don't know what to do, anymore," said Gwen, sinking into the chair opposite Jerry's desk. "You and I both know that sales are down and my people are listless. They aren't motivated and the more I push the less motivated they seem to be. Now even the grapevine says I'm controlling, so it looks pretty bleak from here."

"Sounds like you've backed yourself into a corner. Perhaps you have been a bit too strident . . . too demanding?"

"Perhaps, but that certainly wasn't my intent."

"How is your team development going? Are you letting them into your circle?"

Gwen paused. "My circle?"

"Yeah, your commitment circle."

"I've never heard of it. New management trend? I'll try anything at this point."

"It's not new. I picked it up years ago from a good friend. It was part of The Five Practices of Exemplary Leadership. Basically, it's about learning from everyone. It's about getting out of the box and listening to those who've never been in it. There's more to it, but it makes more sense in context."

"Do you mind sharing it? I could use a new perspective."

Jerry glanced at the clock and crossed quiet time off his mental list. "Let's start with this team you think is yours. You don't really have people, Gwen. No one does. You need to start thinking of the sales team as the people you have the honor of leading. It isn't so much about having followers as joiners. Your job is to provide them the support and resources they need."

"I don't get it. I'm the director. That's got to carry some weight, doesn't it?"

"But Gwen, you're still trying to be the person in charge. Many people in your position lead with their title. It's a common trap. Do you understand the difference between managing and leading?"

"Aren't they one and the same?"

"A lot of people think they are, but they're actually very different. Management is all about things and leadership is about people. Leadership is how you get the management done."

"Wow, three years for an MBA, you'd think someone would have mentioned that."

"Yeah well, this one's on the house, a little on-the-job training. That's where I learned it. You see, Gwen, leadership isn't a title, a position, or really even a level of authority. People tend to mistake decision making for leadership. Some managers think leadership is like a red coat you put on when you want to go out and mingle with the troops. Have you heard the phrase 'managing by wandering around'? If you do it with the right attitude for the right reasons, it can be a great thing. Unfortunately, many so-called leaders do it so that their people can touch the hem of their coat. What's even worse is that they only do it if they have time. And surprise, they hardly ever have the time. I think it has something to do with cold hard fear."

"Fear? Do you think that's why I'm doing what I'm doing?" Gwen asked. She could hear the gentle sssssssss as her confidence seeped from its casings. It reminded her of balloons left over from birthday parties—limp, shriveled, and a bit damp.

"Maybe. Do you feel like you always need to have all the answers for your team? If you do, you're missing the boat. Your job is to nurture and teach. It's an obligation. You're the facilitator for your team, to help them grow as individuals. Like a gardener . . . sowing seeds. That kind of thing."

"But my team doesn't want to grow. They don't want to deal with the problems. I keep laying out the plan and they aren't listening."

"Maybe you're the one not listening, Gwen. It sounds like you spend a lot of time telling them how you would do things, but you don't let them tell you how they would like to do them." Jerry twirled his chair around and reached for a carafe on the credenza beside his desk. He poured them both a glass of water and pressed on. "You never know, they might have a better solution."

"But my way is the right way," blurted Gwen. "It's always been successful."

"Based on the present situation, you'd have a hard time backing that statement up. You know Einstein once said the definition of insanity is doing the same thing over and over again and expecting different results."

"Yeah, but did Einstein ever work in sales?" At least that made Jerry laugh. "I guess you'd have to call me insane. So what do I do now?"

"The friend I spoke of earlier was really a mentor. He once told me leaders see folks not as people who work for them, but as people who choose to work with them as partners. 'Jerry,' he said, 'leaders help people grow into solution sharers, not just problem solvers.' You see, managers always feel that they have to have the answer. Leaders get to ask the questions, knowing that the right one should help others discover the correct answers.' He also told me the higher I climbed on the corporate ladder the more probing and insightful questions I needed to ask."

"I've noticed that about you," said Gwen, and Jerry smiled.

"He said in order to be successful, people need the freedom to learn, to expand their skills and talents. A leader nurtures this kind of behavior. Leaders stretch others, not stress others."

"It's great in theory. It all makes sense, but how do I actually do it?"

❧

The rasp of a weed whacker snapped Gwen's attention back to the present. The gardener had moved on from the pool area and was now trimming a precise path along the stone walkway. Slipping on a pair of flats, she thought about the onsite spa. *A massage*—her shoulders eased just thinking about it. *Aren't massages supposed to increase blood flow to the brain? Free up some brain cells . . . maybe improve my message,* thought Gwen. A massage for a message; definitely add that to the to-do list.

Rounding the first bend, she came upon the gardener. "Hello ma'am," he said with a smile, pulling up to full height and removing a dusty glove. "How are you?"

"Fine, thank you," said Gwen. *I wonder if all of the help is this polite?* "And you?"

"Perfect."

That caught her off guard. "I've never heard anyone say that before," stammered Gwen.

"Well, ma'am, my work is all fun. I have freedom to play. I give tremendous value. And I receive tremendous pay."

"You receive tremendous pay?" Gwen blurted without thinking. *How rude,* she heard her mother's voice. *Never talk money with strangers.*

"Oh, I don't mean the money—I mean I really love my job. I get to be outside all day, where I can see people like you enjoy nature. That's the real pleasure for me. It's the big payoff."

He grinned at her with the most relaxed, genuine smile Gwen had seen in years.

"It must be nice to love your work like that," she sighed enviously. "Can you point me in the direction of the spa?"

"It's just past the pool there, through the red door. Enjoy."

As Gwen turned toward the spa, his response challenged her. *Perfect. Who's perfect? Nobody, that's who.* She glanced over her shoulder, and saw that he was still grinning at her. Shaking her head, she opened the spa door. The cool, airy room beckoned her forward. *Now this is perfect,* she thought.

Sometime later, as she was paying for her massage, Gwen jumped at the chirp of her phone. "Would you mind taking the call outside?" The spa receptionist gestured toward the door. "Sorry," mumbled Gwen, rummaging through her purse. "Hello?"

"Gwen, can I buy you a drink by the pool?"

"I'm researching the spa," she said laughingly. "I'll be right there."

Jerry. He still made her edgy. Maybe it was the timing of the whole thing, with him only a few months into the job and her team on the brink of disaster. She'd seen it before. The new guy pushes the incumbent hard for a few months, creates problems, and then brings in someone from his old company to replace the failure. Was he there to test her and teach her, or to toss her out at the first sign of trouble? He didn't look all that threatening now, though, seated at the poolside bar thumbing the lime wedge deeper into the neck of his Corona.

"What would you like?" Jerry asked, pushing a patio chair out from the table with his foot. "This is a great place," he added. "Did you know I used to live in Arizona when you selected this hotel?"

"I had no idea—I didn't actually pick the place. Patricia in human resources put everything together with Abby Bancroft. The site was her idea. I think people will like it, don't you? And I'd like a chardonnay, please."

"Put that on my tab," said Jerry. "It's on me." He smiled at Gwen. *God, she's tense.* "How's the presentation coming along?"

"I'm only planning to say a few words at the kickoff and then turn it over to Abby, who will be our keynote speaker. My comments will come at the end of the sessions. I'll try to wrap up the information and motivate them a bit."

"You don't sound very motivated yourself. Is there something I can do to help?"

"Just you being here adds value," Gwen said. "It's important for people to know management backs them up."

"Still thinking of me as management, huh," said Jerry, shaking his head. "I guess we didn't really have a chance to finish that conversation. Do you want to pick it up?"

"The Five Practices and that circle thing? You touched on it but we never really got into it in any depth. It's been rattling around in my brain ever since."

"Ah yes, the commitment circle. It is an important part of the leader's toolkit. It will shape your actions. Use it and people are drawn to you."

"Where did it come from?" asked Gwen.

"I didn't invent it, but it's been a real lifesaver for me. Once I really understood it, many other things fell into place. Look,

Gwen, before you can really understand the process, you've got to get your head around the idea of leadership as transformation and management as transaction." Jerry paused and took a long drink. "Many of today's business gurus have it mixed up. They believe management is at the center of the formula and leadership plays a subordinate role to process, planning, and control. That's just nonsense. The real leader knows the difference. His job is to constantly be learning. He needs to constantly improve himself, his teammates, and the organization. The transactions are just tools."

"Hmmmm, interesting—go on, please."

"It's the human connection. People want to feel like they're part of the success, not just used, abused, and tossed overboard. It's all about those Five Practices."

"I could really use some of this in my speech," said Gwen, pulling a pen out of her purse. "Mind if I take a few notes?"

"Be my guest."

"So this Five Practices leadership stuff, is it more of a process or a style?"

"Neither really, it's a way of life. It's a revolution of the mind that changes how we think and act. It happens one person at a time. It's not about a crowd pledging allegiance to it. At its core, leadership is way more than just external behavior. It comes from inside. It's who you are as a person and what you are passionate about."

What am I passionate about? Gwen asked herself. She leaned back in her chair. "So leadership has nothing to do with getting people to do what you *want* them to do?"

"In a way, yes. The word *want* is the key. They're the ones who need to want. You want people to be energized when they come to work. You want them to get excited about shared goals. You want them to join up with you eagerly, not feel like they are being forced. To get that, you need to create an enthusiastic and engaging environment. You need to toss coercion and complacency overboard."

"So how does this connect to the commitment cir—" Jerry's phone leapt from the table blaring out the theme from *Top Gun*. He checked the screen.

"Excuse me for a moment, Gwen, I need to take this call; it's the CEO. Order another drink if you like."

Gwen resisted the temptation to order another glass of wine and turned her chair to face the pool. The gardener was cleaning out a nearby planter box. "Hello," she called out to him without thinking. *Must be the wine.*

"And hello again to you," he said, leaning on his rake.

"Are you still perfect?"

"Most certainly. You seem a bit troubled, though. I'm sorry but I couldn't help overhearing some of your conversation. It reminds me of *my* time in the big chair," he said.

"The big chair?" said Gwen, raising an eyebrow.

"Don't look so surprised, young lady. I wasn't always a groundskeeper. This is more of a hobby for me. Oh no, in my day I was the CEO of a large corporation. I know it's a stretch for the imagination. The work I do here is purely my pleasure."

That's quite a stretch, thought Gwen, eyeing his worn shoes and dusty uniform.

"If I'm not mistaken, you two were talking about some kind of circle."

"Yup, a commitment circle," said Gwen. "It's this leadership technique that my boss, I mean my colleague, swears by—but every time we really get into the meat of it, we're interrupted.

"Sounds like a smart guy, your boss. What's his name?"

"Jerry Allen, and don't call him 'boss.' Gawd, he hates that."

"Me too. When I was back at Applied Diagnostic Design, I liked to be thought of more as a coach or a mentor. I was really into coaching and collaboration before it became all the rage," he said.

"Is that so?" Gwen glanced at Jerry, who thankfully had finished his call and was returning to their table.

"Hey Jerry, how're ya doin'?" The gardener leaned in for a handshake.

"Do I know you?" Jerry glanced over at Gwen, who looked relieved to be off the hook.

"It's been a while, but, yes, without the beard and a few years."

Sam.

"Oh my god. Sam! Sam Arthur!" Jerry lunged forward and grabbed the gardener's outstretched hand. "I can't believe it's you, you old son of a gun. You look great. You look different. You've got a beard. You've got a *rake?*" It didn't line up.

"I'm a groundskeeper here," said Sam. "Two days a week."

"Why?" The question was out before Jerry could quell his curiosity. "I heard you retired with plenty of cash."

"And so I did, Jerry. More than I could ever spend in a lifetime," Sam laughed. "This is just a hobby. It's like I was telling your friend here. It is my pleasure now. I never did get the hang of playing golf, so this is my excuse to play outside. Besides, it lets me stay in touch. My wife and I live up in the mountains in one of those natural 'invisible' houses."

"I just can't believe you're here. I've felt so bad about losing contact. You've always had such an impact on my life. Are you doing any mentoring these days?"

"I still write a bit and twice a week I lecture in the business classes down at U of A. It's kinda fun working with the young ones again. But I think the best learning is right here. You wouldn't believe the kind of things I overhear. People look at a gardener and see a nobody. They look right through me. I'm almost as invisible as my house!" Sam chuckled at the idea.

Gwen felt the flush creep into her cheeks. Sam might as well have been describing her. *Who is this guy?*

"Gwen, this is Sam, my mentor friend from years ago." Swept up in the moment, Jerry had almost forgotten about Gwen.

"Gwen Kelly, nice to meet you." The pieces were starting to fall into place. "So this 'perfect' theme, does that come from your days in the big chair too? You should have heard him introducing himself earlier, Jerry."

"So you're still doing the 'perfect' thing, eh, Sam?"

"Yep, it always throws people. I like to change it up a bit. Get a little something other than 'fine' out of people."

"Sam's always trying new things," said Jerry. "Always working to get people thinking. I still think about things that you taught me, Sam. In fact, Gwen and I were just going over The Five Practices and your coaching process."

"The circle thing is *his?*" *This is crazy. I'm taking advice from a gardening CEO,* thought Gwen.

"Oh, absolutely," said Jerry. "Sam invented it."

"I wouldn't go that far," said Sam. "The Commitment Circle is my concept. It's how I look at The Five Practices, which sprang from the groundbreaking research of my mentors, Jim Kouzes and Barry Posner."

Gwen pulled out a third chair. "In that case, have a seat, because neither of you are getting out of here."

CHAPTER 3

The Lone Stranger
Monday—3:29 PM

As Charlie Verona's plane bounced its way through the thunderclouds over Tucson, he sipped his coffee and thought back to the two-day, somewhat stormy, workshop in Chicago he had wrapped up just a few hours earlier. He couldn't believe how the guy who'd hired him could have been so clueless.

"So, credibility is about believability. People will join with you when they know they can count on you. Your 'walk the talk' reputation precedes you," Charlie had said, surveying the room. "It's tough to earn and easy to lose." A cell phone shrilled from the back, interrupting his train of thought. "You know my policy," Charlie raised his voice. "Turn 'em off or put 'em on stun."

But without turning a hair, the CEO had fished into his jacket pocket. "This is John," he'd said, plugging in his earpiece and turning his back to the room.

Charlie recalled feeling his jaw drop. *Are you kidding me?* It was incredible. Continuing the conversation, John had scraped his chair back and stood up, shuffled his papers together, and walked out. Credibility and respect left with him. At least Charlie had been able to salvage the situation in the room, by—rightly or wrongly—using the CEO's behavior as an example of poor leadership. That was Charlie's style: confrontational and unconventional. But he got results, great results.

Stories like that were the ones Charlie lived for. He loved going into a damaged workplace and turning the world upside down. *This is the whole point of The Five Practices,* he'd thought, glancing around the room. To show people what real leadership was about. Still, if he couldn't get through to the guys at the top, like John, there wasn't much hope.

Charlie chortled aloud, making his seatmates a bit nervous as he recalled his confrontation with John. "Have you got a few minutes to talk about your results from the LPI?" he'd asked. He loved how The Leadership Practices Inventory could show people in black and white how their behavior affected the workplace.

John was visibly angry at being confronted. "I don't put much value in surveys like that," he'd said, bordering on hostility. "I'm more of a take-charge guy."

"Why don't you take some time to think about it tonight and then let's get together for breakfast," Charlie had said.

A different John met Charlie at the hotel coffee shop the next morning.

"I told my wife about you last night. About the report and how the moron—sorry—who was leading the seminar thought

I was a control freak," John had said, fiddling with the lid on his coffee cup.

Moron, thought Charlie. *Add that to the list.*

"And my wife, she just stares at me and says, 'Uh-huh,' like it's no big surprise. So, I ask her if our son feels the same way and she rolls her eyes at me! I can't believe this. I call my son into the living room, he's twelve, and I tell him about the report results. I even define 'controlling' to make sure he knows exactly what I'm talking about. Then he tears up and says, 'Dad, you hurt my feelings all the time.'" John had paused for so long Charlie could see the transformation in his posture. This man was defeated. "I can't keep doing this, Charlie. I know I've been on a slippery slope for a while now. I can see it now clearly. The stress is getting to me. My choices are getting in the way. I'm treating my employees like dirt. I'm treating my wife like dirt. I'm hurting my son. I'm just not sure what to do next." It was going to be a long road back, but at least John was now moving toward the right on ramp.

Transformations, even seemingly overnight ones like John's, don't happen every day, thought Charlie. Usually a lot of thought preceded them, along with frustration, anger, and disappointment. But it was epiphanies like this that made up for the constant travel, the airline food and the shuttles. *Well, maybe not the shuttles.*

Charlie's mind shifted to the week ahead. So many people treated these off-site training sessions like a vacation, trotting out their 'workshop' behavior during the day and then hitting the town at night. Would the teams from Advanced Biomolecular Pharmaceuticals and American Laboratory for Molecular Research be any different? *Clever idea,* he thought, scheduling a joint offsite for competing organizations now collaborating on new drug technology. Going to make for some interesting dynamics, that's for damn sure. But would they really get into the content or would they just fill in the workbook, 'dialogue' with their colleagues to impress the facilitator, and then take a pass when it was time for a little life-changing behavior?

Although Perfect Leadership Consulting contracted with several speakers and workshop leaders, they rarely trod the trails together. This week would be different, though. It had been two months since he and Abby crossed paths. She was his supervisor in an independent contractor sort of way, but they shared a common unspoken bond. He knew he was attracted to her, but what could happen? They only saw each other a few times a year. Not exactly the best way to build a personal relationship. And what were her thoughts about him? Purely professional, I'm sure, he thought. Although, there was that come-hither flick of a smile last time they met. What did that mean?

Charlie loved his work. In fact, he fancied himself to be a bit of a leadership cowboy, roaming the country and sharing his brand of white-Stetson justice with the mixed-up managers of the world. *But even cowboys get lonely.* He couldn't wait to grab a drink and swap stories, catch up on life, spend some time together before they packed up and rode off to different cities once again.

As the La Mariposa Resort & Spa rolled into view, Charlie felt the exhaustion of dingy hotels, fast food, and public transportation slipping away. *Now these guys know how to do it up right,* he thought, taking in the view.

Once in his room, Charlie grabbed the phone and asked the operator to dial the number for Abby's suite. He needed to get his room assignment for the morning. He needed to review the pre-work. Charlie was meticulous with room setup. It created the ambience and environment he needed to work his magic and he didn't like participants to see behind the curtain. His "Wizard of Oz complex," that's what his agent called it.

When Abby didn't answer the phone, Charlie knew where to find her: Checking out the conference rooms for the workshop sessions, or checking out the bar.

CHAPTER 4

The Games Begin
Monday–7:07 PM

Joe Vanderson hunched over the hotel bed and pulled a sport coat out of his suitcase. Everything underneath was wrinkled. He had no idea where Nora had kept the iron, if she'd even left the iron. She'd moved out a few days earlier, and he could still hear the door slamming, her BMW roaring out the driveway. He hadn't told anyone. Thirty-two years and now it was over. His empty suitcase fit neatly in the closet. He'd need a storage unit for the emotional baggage.

He stepped onto his private patio and lit a cigarette with a quick flick of his antique lighter. Drawing on the slim sliver of death, he thought about quitting. *Not now, though.* Stress was too much already. Smoking seemed to ease the pain. Settling his six-foot, rail-thin frame into the lounge chair, Joe flicked his cigarette ash onto the floor and looked for an ashtray. *Gawd, I hate these retreat things,* he said to himself. *All that bloody kumbaya crap.* Too touchy-feely for his taste. Besides, there was much to do back at the office and even more to do back at home. His life was in shambles and the lines on his craggy face showed it. He should have seen it coming. Things hadn't been the same since they'd lost their investments in the dot-com crash. Ego had kept him from selling his stock. *No sir. Going to ride that stock and my retirement plan into the sunset.*

Money didn't matter much to Nora. At least that's what she told him. But it was the beginning of the end. She'd stopped taking his crap, stopped letting his words slide by with their hidden assumptions. *Maybe if there'd been kids,* he thought, but they'd never been able to have them. Disappointing, but it was OK. *I mean, it wasn't really my fault.* He'd heard through the grapevine one of his flings got pregnant. He wasn't sure it was his, but the idea stroked his ego. Sometimes he wondered if she'd gone through with the pregnancy, if he did have a child, but she'd never called. And if he really thought too much about it, the guilt was overwhelming. He loved Nora. The flings were just crutches, a little something on the side to cheer him up and keep him going.

He was still smarting over the CEO rejection. *I know more about growing pharmaceutical sales than anyone,* he thought. But the Board of Directors thought differently. Now he didn't know if he should stay. *I don't even fit in anymore, and the new guys are driving me crazy.* No respect for the establishment, the people who've worked their way up. The new HR Queen was young enough to be his daughter, and she was behaving as if she was his boss! *Beautiful, sure, but a bit of a corporate slut if you ask me.* She needed to be knocked down a peg or two. And Gordon the Great Murphy, well, who wanted to spend two days "team building" with the guy who got the job you deserved?

What Joe hated most about Gordon was his servant leadership bullshit. He'd been shaking things up from day one. Asking people for ideas, organizing brainstorming sessions, and spending time with everybody—*nobody's going to take that kind of leadership seriously,* Joe thought. You had to be the decider. The tough one. You open yourself up to other people and soon they're walking all over you. What was the point of being CEO if you were going to let other people help you run the show? *This whole offsite was Gordon's idea and a damn waste of time.* Joe was already angry about the pre-work that they'd assigned and that "360-degree leadership inventory" thing was ridiculous. Why in the world would you ever give your subordinates the opportunity to rag on you in public? *Who cares what they think?* It just didn't make sense. Nothing made sense anymore. Maybe Nora was right. He needed a shrink. She'd asked him to get help a few years back when his father passed away but he'd never gone.

Joe had loved his father and feared him at the same time. He could give a whipping like nobody's business. Joe had been on the receiving end of a few belt straps more than once.

His old man had started out selling newspapers and shining shoes but eventually built a small grocery wholesale business. He was self-employed all of his life. *He'd never make it today,* thought Joe. Everything's gone high-tech and corporate. Impersonal. There was no time for leaning over the counter, getting face to face with your customers. His father was a master at interpersonal relationships. He'd employed more than twenty people and treated them all like family. *If anything, that was his weakness,* thought Joe. He'd tried to father them all. And there wasn't much left for his sons at the end of the day.

His mom had a religious compulsion for volunteer work keeping her busy and his older brother James had fallen from grace years ago. Diagnosed with lung cancer, he was too busy dying to call. *Going to smoke himself to death,* Joe thought, as he smashed his own cigarette into the ashtray while simultaneously lighting another.

In the early 1970s, when his parents had planned to take an extended vacation and volunteer halfway around the world, his dad's employees threw him a roast. Joe and his brother James were invited to attend. *That was the first night that I remember feeling proud of him,* thought Joe. These men, unskilled workers who would never stand up in front of a group, raised hands one after the other to roast and toast this man and his life. He was their leader. He had saved them from financial ruin with small loans. He had kept them out of trouble, off the streets, out of jail. They were honored to work for him, honored to have been chosen by him. But what did honor get you in the end?

A bed in the veterans' nursing home. That's where he died. The memories washed over Joe. He'd made it a point to visit at least twice a week, smuggling in two beers. It was really their only connection; drinking beer and small talk. Joe's dad had worked six days a week. On Sundays, they went to church and to visit family. They'd never played together, never gone to ball games, never worked on an old jalopy. They'd never even played a game of catch. *I should have taken a ball to the home and thrown a few to him in his wheelchair,* he thought. Another lost opportunity.

He had to stop thinking about it. He rubbed his temples and exhaled. Watching his father succumb to the pain, his quick and shallow breathing, the vacant look in his eyes, it was too much.

The phone rang, jerking him out of the past. Joe choked back a sob and retreated into the cool of the room. "This is Joe," he coughed, disguising the catch in his voice.

"Glad I caught you. Listen, I'm trying to round up a team for dinner at Jake's. I'd like you to join us." It was Gordon. Already starting in on the team building. *That man should have been a cruise director.*

Joe sighed. He couldn't think of an excuse. "What time?"

"Eight o'clock. The team will meet in the lobby."

"All right, see you then." Joe dropped the phone into the cradle and looked at his watch. Forty minutes. Enough time for a cocktail. He grabbed his jacket and headed for the door. Let the games begin.

PART TWO

Connections

CHAPTER 5

Yoda Is My Gardener
Monday–4:57 PM

Charlie finally tracked down Abby, who was talking with some of the staff outside the seminar rooms in preparation for the days to come. Charlie could feel his heart quicken as he walked along the hallway toward her. She looked as good as ever, maybe better. He called out her name so as not to startle her. "Hey, Abby, how was your flight?"

Abby spun around quickly and smiled, "Charlie, great to see you." She held out her hand and grasped Charlie's but then leaned forward and gave him a one-armed hug. Charlie reciprocated.

"I'm just going over a few things here for tomorrow." Abby turned to the two La Mariposa staff members and thanked them for their time.

"So, are you ready?" she asked Charlie.

"I'm always ready," replied Charlie, immediately regretting what he felt could have been construed as an inappropriate double entendre. "Let's change some lives," he added to try to bring it back to the business theme.

"OK then," Abby said, noticing but choosing to ignore Charlie's less-than-subtle come-on. "I'll catch you in a little while. Let's meet in the lobby bar. You go ahead and check out your workshop room." With a slightly forced smile, she left Charlie and headed toward the outdoor bar.

"Abby. Abby, over here!" Sam called from the poolside tables.

Abby grinned. "Sam, great to see you. Jerry, hi, it's been a while. Nice outfit, Sam! You said you were dabbling in the hotel business, but really? As the gardener? I don't believe we've met," she said, turning to Gwen and extending her hand.

"Gwen Kelly. I'm the director of sales at Advanced Biomolecular Pharmaceuticals."

"Nice to meet you."

Jerry motioned to the chair and flagged down the bartender.

"What can I get for you, madam?"

"How about a club soda with extra lime. Thanks."

"So I'm assuming that the three of you are already acquainted," said Gwen. *That's just perfect,* she thought, *a nice little "in" club.*

"Well indirectly, yes," said Abby. "Both Jerry and I have had the privilege of studying under the leadership guru that is Sam."

"Yes," replied Jerry in mock seriousness, "we are but young Jedi knights. Sam is our Yoda."

"Flatter me, you do." Sam laughed. "Abby was one of my first serious pupils and now she's carrying on The Five Practices leadership message. The student has become the master, so to speak."

"Ah, you're too kind," replied Abby. "Actually, Gwen, years ago I attended one of Sam's goal-setting sessions and it really shook me up. Got me thinking. I was heavy into the publishing business, but my life wasn't really lining up with my goals. Sam helped me make some changes."

"All for the better. All for the better, Abby."

"Well, I couldn't have done it without you. What's with the rake?"

"It's just another hobby. Keeps me out of trouble," replied Sam.

"So is that how you got into the leadership training business, Abby?" Gwen asked. "Because of Sam?"

"Absolutely. After that goal-setting session, which incidentally I had organized because I thought it was my team whose goals were off, my conversations with Sam led to a new business venture of marketing trainers and speakers. I put together this pilot session for Sam to make a presentation. About two weeks before the workshop, he landed a huge account in Texas and had to cancel."

"Really let Abby down," said Sam with a sheepish smile. "But it all worked out in the end."

"True, but at the time, I was really in a bind. While I'm scrambling to find another speaker for the event, Sam calls back and says, 'Why don't you do it? I'll send you all my materials and my slides.' Two weeks later, I'm standing in front of people I barely know, teaching stuff I know nothing about with skills I didn't even know I had."

"I knew she could do it," said Sam with a wink to Gwen. "She was a natural."

"It went a lot better than I expected, and after the nerves wore off, I actually had a good time. Before I knew it, I was doing one or two workshops a month. But it was kind of a side job. I didn't really think all that much about it until I was working with a group and a fellow helped me carry my equipment out to my car. As we're walking down the hallway he said, 'Thanks,' and I said something like, 'No problem, I'm happy to be with you folks today.' He must have picked up on something because he stopped and stared at me for a moment." Abby continued. "'No, you don't understand,' he said. 'The work we did today was very important. The conversations we had changed my life.' And I thought about that all the way home. Those words lit my passion pilot light. I had always thought that journalism was my calling, and it was, for a while, but when I finally felt the true impact of what I was supposed to do next, it was unbelievable."

"Wow, you're intensely into this stuff," said Gwen. "I can see you really love your work. You must be proud, Sam. Seeing as you started all of this."

"My legacy is deep," Sam responded. "Jerry, Abby, Gordon, Charlie, and a few hundred other close personal friends are all out spreading the word. They've all found their voices. It's their story now. Who knows Gwen, maybe you'll be next."

"Who are Gordon and Charlie?" Gwen asked.

"Charlie Verona is one of the other facilitators for this week and Gordon Murphy is the CEO at ALMR. You'll meet both of them tomorrow," answered Abby. "But just keep in mind, Gwen, Sam is the conductor, we are just the instruments," Abby said.

Sam rose from the table and gave a deep bow, "I am but a humble gardener."

Jerry laughed, "Sure Sam. You're just a gardener; a gardener who is planting activist seeds all around the world.

Abby glanced at her watch. "Speaking of Charlie, I'm supposed to meet up with him again in a few minutes. I'll see you two at the first session tomorrow, if not before. Sam, it was great to see you. Let's grab some lunch while I'm in town. Talk some business."

"Yes, Abby. Anytime." Sam rose to leave.

"Oh no you don't," said Gwen. "You two still owe me a commitment circle conversation."

"Let's say we move this conversation inside," said Jerry. "Can you join us at the coffee shop, Sam? I think Gwen should hear about the commitment circle from the man who made it possible."

"Give me a minute to put away my tools and I'll be right there."

"The hotel won't mind you sitting with us, will they?" Gwen stammered. La Mariposa didn't seem like the kind of place that'd approve of their gardeners having coffee with the guests.

"Oh no, the management knows I come and go pretty much as I please. As long as I do what I have signed up to do, how and when I do it is up to me."

Jerry chuckled. That was classic Sam. He even had the hotel eating out of his hand.

Light My Fire
Monday—5:42 PM

"Let's be clear from the start—leadership isn't just for famous figureheads, Gwen. It's tough stuff, but anyone at any level in life is up to it. They just have to find their internal fire and it ignites with knowing what is important to them," Sam began as he settled into his seat.

"That's right," added Jerry. "It's a personal and crucial choice because in order to really lead you have to know who you are and what matters to you. It has to come from the inside."

"Every truly great leader struggles with the question of whether or not they are up to the task," Sam continued. But it's passion and their struggle that helps them create their legacy, their masterpiece if you will."

"Sam's a big proponent of masterpieces," said Jerry. "Whenever I was at a turning point, he would ask me if I was painting my masterpiece or merely daubing at the edges of someone else's paint-by-numbers portrait."

"I sort of stole that from Gordon Mackenzie, from his book *Orbiting the Giant Hairball*," confessed Sam.

"That's quite a title," said Gwen with laugh.

"It's quite a book. Made a real impression on me," Sam replied. "Mackenzie wrote, 'You have a masterpiece inside of you and if you go to your grave without painting your masterpiece, it will not get painted. No one else can paint it . . . only you.' People spend too much time trying to keep up with trends and techniques and not enough time listening to those little voices in their heads."

"Really?" laughed Gwen. "Are you suggesting insanity as a new leadership tool?"

"No, no. I'm talking about those little voices that remind you of your childhood dreams. The ones that niggle at the back of your mind asking, 'What would you really like to do if only . . . if only you had the time . . . if only you had the money?'"

Gwen leaned forward, propping her chin up with her hand. She'd squashed that voice so many times she'd forgotten what it sounded like. "I've never really put much emphasis on my regrets."

"Then you might be missing your masterpiece," said Sam.

Sam's words echoed in Gwen's mind. *Am I really missing it? Is that why my team is falling apart, why my career is falling apart? Maybe I'm just not passionate about sales anymore.* She thought about Eastridge Executive Recruitment. She was supposed to call this week about the interview they were setting up. *Maybe a new opportunity would add a little passion to my leadership,* she thought. Either way, she knew she wanted to hear more from Sam. Jerry and Abby seemed to have it all together and Sam seemed to be the source of knowledge. "Sam, I hope you don't think I'm being too forward, but I'd like to spend more time with you."

"I'm sure we can find some time. I'm always up for a little one-on-one coaching."

"Actually," Gwen paused. Listen to the little voice? Don't listen to the little voice? "Actually, I was hoping you might be able to share some of this at our workshops this week. I mean, if that works for you. If you're still doing that kind of thing."

Sam relaxed into the smile that had struck Gwen earlier in the day. "If it works for you, it works for me. Way to challenge, Gwen."

"Excuse me?"

"Ah, that's more of Sam's mentors' wisdom . . . the umbrella for everything else," said Jerry. "The Five Practices: *Model the Way, Inspire a Shared Vision, Challenge the Process, Enable Others to Act,* and *Encourage the Heart.* Seriously Sam, you should write a book too."

"In due time, Jerry. It will be in your hands before you know it. For now, I rely on The Five Practices from Kouzes and Posner's *The Leadership Challenge.* Their research was foundational for me."

"Leave it to you, Sam. Always giving credit where credit is due. Total integrity." Jerry turned to Gwen. "As a leader, Gwen, you need to Model the Way, with your integrity out front just like that because credibility matters. You have to walk the talk. Connect your hips to your lips."

"Cute."

"Hey, people remember things that rhyme. You need to Inspire a Shared Vision because your voice matters. Your words and your stories motivate those around you. You need to Challenge the Process because your actions matter. And you need to Enable Others to Act and Encourage their Hearts because your gift and gratitude matters. We all have something to share in this world and we all deserve praise."

"And not just at work. Everywhere. Our leadership matters because we matter—and we need to focus on what matters," said Sam.

"Make sense, Gwen?" asked Jerry.

"Yeah, it's just a lot to take in, to process, you know." Gwen paused. "I don't know, Jerry, I just don't know if I'm ready for your idea of leadership. I mean the way that you and Sam describe it, it seems like the kind of thing you'd expect from Martin Luther King Jr., or Gandhi."

Arranging to have Sam take part in the workshops had been remarkably easy. A quick call to Abby and he was on board. Jerry was still digesting the idea when the senior ABP sales staff gathered for dinner at Anthony's on Skyline Blvd. He'd wanted to reconnect with Sam for years and now the timing couldn't be better, for him or for Gwen.

Jerry loved Anthony's, with its great valley views. He'd brought more than a few dates here back in the day. Tonight there was a large group of what appeared to be fathers and daughters in the middle of the main room; probably some type of a sorority event. Geez, how many years would it be before he'd be attending these dinners with Jennifer? She was already a high school freshman. Only a few more years and he'd be one of those dads beaming down the table at his beautiful girl, engaging in a comical debate over which dad would be stuck with the sizable check. He missed his kids. He excused himself. "Going to call home before it's too late," he said, leaning toward Gwen. "Why don't you go ahead and tell the team about Sam. Prepare them for the change of plans."

Gwen bit her lip. It had seemed like such a good idea at the time, but now, glancing around the table, she wasn't so sure. "Can I have everybody's attention for a few minutes? I'd like to run over some details for the upcoming sessions." Oh, oh. Was that little voice getting louder? "First of all, I'd like to say that I'm really excited about the next few days. We've had a rough couple of years. I think this offsite is exactly what we need to get back on track." She sensed the stifling of eye rolls. "I also added an additional speaker to our vision strategy session. His name is Sam Arthur and I think you're really going to connect with his message. I've already spent some time with him today. I think he's a perfect choice for us."

CHAPTER 7

Suck or Succeed
Monday—5:36 PM

Charlie scanned the long, wood-paneled hotel bar. Abby was perched at a corner table, surrounded by the contents of her briefcase. "Hey, Abby."

"You look a bit worn around the edges, Charlie," Abby said with a smile.

"Tough week," said Charlie. "Just flew in from a two-day in Chicago."

"Sit, sit. What are you drinking?"

"Ketel One martini up and dirty," Charlie said to the waiting bartender.

"Shaken or stirred, sir?"

"I don't care what you do with it first—just make sure you get all of it in the glass," Charlie shot back, laughing. "So Abby, what's the deal with this week? Do we really have two pharmaceutical companies in the same hotel at the same time holding joint workshops?"

"That's right," Abby replied. "Do you remember when we did those combination sessions for Star Macro Systems? Well, this is another take on that format, only this time we're running it with two separate companies instead of two departments in the same company. ABP and ALMR are working on some of the same technologies, so they wanted to partner their sales teams. We're going to do separate sessions with each group and then bring them together a few times to get to know each other."

"And it will give us a chance to connect and do some bonding of our own," Charlie blurted.

Again with the double entendres, Abby thought. *What does he think he's doing?* Didn't he know about Dennis and the ring and the . . . *no,* she said to herself. *Of course he doesn't.* She hadn't told him. She hadn't told anyone.

"I see from the schedule you've got me working primarily with the team from ALMR," Charlie said, catching himself again. "Two days of The Leadership Challenge Workshop with their large group and then the executives are going to spend a day to do some internal work? What's their story?"

"They're a great group," said Abby. "I've known the CEO, Gordon Murphy, for a number of years. He just joined them last year and he's looking to make some changes to his executive team. Most of them are keepers, but there's this one guy really causing problems."

"How so?" Charlie sipped his martini and leaned back in his chair.

"This guy—Joe Vanderson—has been around the company forever. He was even a candidate for the CEO spot that eventually went to Gordon. That left a nasty aftertaste. He's been a thorn in Gordon's side ever since."

"Sour grapes, huh?"

"Yeah, but there's more to it. Apparently, he was a terrific salesman who kept being promoted higher and higher, but he never really got any training and it shows. The guy's a micro-micromanager. He's just killing the team. Plus, Gordon is concerned with his ethics. A few things just aren't lining up."

"And Gordon doesn't want to see the whole thing go down in flames?"

"Exactly. Anywhere money is involved, like sales, it's just getting easier and easier to slip. I'm not sure why that is, but it's an ethical concern. How are you addressing that in the field?" Abby asked.

"I always ask people where their line is; the line that marks the ethical gap. Ask them if they even know when they've crossed it. Like, is it OK to shred documents that you know you shouldn't when the boss insists? Is your mortgage worth more than your integrity?"

"Ah, your *suck versus success* line?"

"That's the one," replied Charlie. "We've got all kinds of so-called leaders doing the walk of shame, charged with this or that violation. I'm never really shocked by it, but the number still surprises me from time to time."

"I don't know if this guy from Gordon's group will ever go to jail, but he's going to get himself escorted out of the building if he doesn't get his act together. He's your focus for this week,

Charlie. I want you to figure out how to reach this guy and help Gordon begin to really create a community with his team."

"What else do you know about him?"

Abby shuffled through the files on the table. "Some pretty nasty behavior. I've got a few examples here for you to review. You can keep these. Just know that nobody trusts him and that reputation appears to be well earned, according to comments in these files.

"And to top it off, the guy doesn't seem to want friends. His team tried to surprise him for his birthday with a little at-work celebration and he yelled at them. Told them to stop wasting their time; threw out all the streamers and balloons."

"And you assigned this guy to me because . . . why? Sounds like a guy with a penchant for fear and humiliation."

"No kidding. Behavioral researchers are all over fear in the workplace right now. They know bullies love to make their subordinates squirm. It's all about power. Bullies make people sick. Watching the stress wash over others creates great pleasure for the fear-mongers."

"That's pretty serious stuff," said Charlie. "I can see why Gordon is concerned."

"I know. Gordon needs Joe to change his behavior or move on. And you're going to be critical in the process, Charlie. You've had great experience with this type of situation before. That's why I put you with this particular group. You have that 'in your face' approach that gets to the point quickly. It's going to be messy; there's no way around it."

"Emotional, too. No one likes to be told they're not making the cut. I think it's going to take a lot of coaching. Not just with Joe, but with the entire team. We've obviously got a lot of working wounded on our hands."

"You know, we should probably touch base with Gordon. He's going to be in all of Joe's sessions. He'll be able to give you more information than I've got here. Let me see if he's available to join us. Can I get you another while I'm up?" She motioned toward Charlie's empty glass.

"You paying?"

"For what you've got coming, it's the least I can do."

Gordon reached for the phone, untangling himself from the comforter. He'd hoped for a nap before dinner. "Hello, Gordon Murphy. Abby, hi. . . . Doing well . . . thanks. . . . No immediate plans. I've got dinner with the team later tonight. . . . Mmm hmmm. . . . Sure. Give me a few minutes to change and I'll be right there." He slid the receiver back onto the cradle. *Good-bye nap.*

As he strode across the patio toward the hotel entrance, he thought about Joe. *Tricky business. It's going to be push-come-to-shove time with him.* However, he wanted to avoid the slash-and-burn mentality that so many others employed. *He has experience like nobody's business, but his attitude is awful.* If only Joe could get his act together. *This Charlie fellow had better be as good in person as he is on paper,* he muttered. He'd know in a minute.

"Hi, Abby, it's great to see you again. I assume you're Charlie. I've heard a lot about you," Gordon said, approaching them with his hand extended. "Most of it good," he added.

Charlie shook his hand and introduced himself. He enjoyed the bad-boy reputation Gordon mentioned. Though he did wish he could have had Abby to himself.

"Now, don't get me wrong. I think you might be the right guy for our situation. I hope so, anyway. It's just that your reputation precedes you. Do you really push people's buttons in your sessions?" Gordon didn't miss a beat.

"I'm told I do. Sometimes it takes a candy bar to get people to open up. Sometimes it takes a crow bar. I'm flexible."

Gordon laughed. "Touché."

"Sometimes," Charlie said as he stroked his glass, "we get groups that say they want to be shaken and stirred. But they don't really mean it. They'd much rather be coddled and comforted."

"We don't let them get away with that," said Abby. "We send them Charlie. He mixes it up a bit."

"I like to throw out 'thought grenades' during my talks. Sometimes they go off immediately and other times they might take hours, days, weeks, or even years. But eventually they do go off and people get the point."

"Speaking of the point," Abby interrupted, "Gordon, we'd like some more details about Joe."

"Joe is . . . ahh . . . a piece of work." There was really no other way to say it. At least in polite company.

"Yeah, Abby's already pointed that out. But what I want to know is, what's his personality like? Sounds like he's passive-aggressive."

"No, it's more than that. He's *aggressive-aggressive*—and in a shrewd sort of way. He has his master's in 'lipotage'—you know, the kind of verbal sabotage that can undermine everything. I mean, he's read all the leadership and management books. He knows all the right words, even quotes them back to the rest of us. But his attitude and behavior are completely out of step with our organization," Gordon hesitated. How much did they really need to know? "His management style is more 'who can we burn?' than 'what can we learn?'" he added. "I'm sure he's already met with an attorney."

With that, Gordon's phone began to buzz. Excuse me," he said, pushing his chair back and getting up from the table. "It's my assistant. I need to take this. I'll get back to you on all this, Charlie. Good to meet you."

Oh damn, Abby thought as she forced another smile. "Good luck."

"See ya, Gordon," Charlie said. "Be well."

Should I tell Charlie about Dennis now? Abby wondered. Or perhaps it was best not to say anything. What if Charlie's intentions were all in her imagination?

"I should be going, too," she said. "I need to review my notes before the session tomorrow, and I thought I'd check out the spa."

Was that a look of disappointment on Charlie's face?

"Put the tab on the expense account," she said. "See you in the morning."

CHAPTER 8

Pyramids Amid Denial
Monday—7:46 PM

J oe strode up the stairs to the Desert Garden Lounge on the mezzanine level. He really needed a drink. Maybe two. He motioned to the bartender and ordered a scotch and soda. *If you can't beat the memories, drown 'em,* he thought.

"Joe, I thought I saw you come in." *Damn.* It was Gordon. *No escaping him now.* "How was your flight in?"

"Great," replied Joe, turning back to the bar. *Can't the stupid bastard see I don't want company?* It was bad enough he had to join the group for dinner. Couldn't he at least let him drink in peace? Gordon sat down on the stool beside Joe and ordered a plain tonic with a twist.

"How's your room?"

"Great," said Joe robotically. "I really like the view."

"How did you do on the workshop pre-work? Did you get it all done? From what I understand, this Charlie Verona is a stickler for pre-work."

Joe took a drink and grabbed a handful of nuts from the dish near his glass. "It's probably all talk. These workshop guys are all the same; happy-talkers or charlatans. A waste of company time and money, if you ask me." *Which you didn't,* thought Joe, glowering.

"Charlie says he's not like that, Joe," Gordon said. "I actually just met him, but his reputation appears to back him up. He insists people who come to his sessions take them seriously enough to follow through on the pre-work. He hates it when people don't do the work and then give his workshops poor marks."

"Calm down. I did the work, all fifteen pages of it. Of course, I had to rearrange my schedule to fit it in and now I'm behind on other projects, which is only made worse by the fact you've got us out here at team-building camp for the next two days."

"I'm sorry you feel that way," Gordon replied. "You've never found anything in offsite sessions that was worth taking home with you?"

"I've tried some of the things, but they never work."

"Give me an example?" Gordon was curious. The idea that Joe had ever tried something new surprised him.

"I went to a session once about letting your staff be more involved in planning their celebrations. This was about ten years ago. I was looking for a way to bring the guys together. I asked some of my staff to find out what people wanted to do to celebrate. They were excited about the idea and put together a suggestion box for people to share their ideas. After a few weeks, they came back to me and said people wanted gift certificates to McDonald's and a movie so they could go in small groups when they had time."

"Sounds harmless," said Gordon. "What happened?"

"I was really kind of insulted. I mean here I wanted to do something special for them, and they just wanted fast food and cheap entertainment. I decided to go one better. I called a friend who owned a trendy restaurant downtown and made reservations for the entire group for lunch. Then I booked the movie theater for a private afternoon showing of a film festival winner."

"Were they surprised?"

"Oh yeah. But not like you'd think. Lunch was a disaster. Most of them had never been to such a fancy restaurant. They didn't know how to act, or what forks to use, and everyone was really edgy. I was so embarrassed."

"But surely they enjoyed the movie?"

"After the restaurant incident I thought, if we could only get through the movie without a problem, I could salvage the rest of the afternoon. But they hated the movie. They were like little kids. 'Is it over yet?' That sort of thing. At least they liked the popcorn."

"So I guess the moral of the story is when you ask people what they want, and they tell you, you should do what they ask," said Gordon with a slight chuckle.

Joe was stunned. Did the man have no sympathy? *He asked for an example. I delivered. Now he's dumping the whole thing back on me. There's no pleasing him.* Anger tugged at the muscles in his forehead. A low-grade migraine was already creeping under his skull.

"You know, Joe, I can relate to what you're saying here." Gordon—realizing his error—was determined to salvage the moment. "My business upbringing was probably very similar to yours. When I first got into the corporate arena, everything employees did was to serve the people at the top . . . the president and every person in a position of authority up the chain of command. It was the pyramid-style management approach with the followers as nobodies at the bottom and the titled leaders as somebodies at the top. It was command and control at its finest.

"When I got my first job, I used to watch the executives come and go every day. They'd all arrive around nine or ten in the morning, and then leave for power lunches at noon. Then it was back to the office by two, usually a little weak in the knees from two or three martinis, to do meetings and paperwork until five. Then it was off to the club for a round of golf or a round of drinks before heading home to the little woman—who'd have dinner on the table and pearls around her neck. I couldn't wait to grow up to be an executive."

"It looks like you got your wish," said Joe. "It doesn't get much better than CEO of a growing pharmaceutical company."

"No, it doesn't," said Gordon. "But the corporate climate has really changed. As I moved up the ladder, people started expecting more. Performance reviews were born, only they called them 'management by objectives' back then. I was angry. I wanted my turn at the country club lifestyle. And now that I'm an executive, the pyramid has completely reversed. Instead of being at the top of the pyramid, the leaders are at the bottom and those who report to them are at the top. That's the whole idea of servant leadership. Everything the leader does is to support the work at the top."

"That may be true of where you've come from, but it doesn't work like that at ALMR," said Joe. "We've still got bottom-dwellers feeding the corporate structure at the top." Sometimes Gordon was so naive. *Well, I'm not going to follow him around like a duckling, no matter how many pyramids he builds.*

"You're probably right," Gordon was quick to reply. "They haven't flipped over for us everywhere yet, and they didn't always do so in my previous experiences either. You should hear what happened to my team at my last company."

This ought to be good, thought Joe. He'd listen to any story where Gordon the Great hadn't come out on top.

Gordon pressed on. "We were at a major meeting where awards were being given out and I was fairly new to the organization. The executive vice president got up to the platform and shouted, 'The third place honor for most improved division goes to Utah.' There's cheering and groaning from those who won or figured they'd lost. 'Second place goes to Colorado.'" Gordon paused for effect. "First place was a really big deal because all the vice presidents and divisional sales directors received an all-expanse-paid trip to Hawaii with their spouses."

"So did you win?" Joe grudgingly asked.

"Not a chance," Gordon responded. "The California division was in terrible shape when they hired me. They were even thinking about shutting down the office. I was supposed to come in, turn it all around, fire the deadweight and hire a new team. This big award ceremony was just a couple weeks into the job. When Arizona walked away with first prize, my team was at such a low point that they didn't even react. I knew I had to take some action." He paused, looking back in time.

"As I said, I was supposed to fire most of the existing team, but I could see raw talent in a lot of them, even though they didn't have much of a reputation for excellence in their respective departments. I kept most of them, moved them into different roles, and used their natural abilities and 'maverick' assertiveness to get us back on track. Once I secured the right talent and resources for the job, I stepped back and left the managers alone as much as possible. Man, they hated that at first. They'd been so micromanaged, always getting spoon-fed the answers, never having to think for themselves. But once they realized they had the ability to answer their own questions, they really embraced the idea."

"So how does this fit into the pyramid thing?" asked Joe.

"I'm getting there. After a few weeks, one of the managers comes into my office and asks if they can try for the award next year. This is one of the same guys who could hardly engage the year before. I told him California might not be included in the list of eligible divisions because of our failures in the past. But that just fueled his desire. I told him if we were going to aim for it, we should aim for the top, and that I would do anything I could to support their efforts. To make a long story short, a year later we walked away with first place. The team went crazy! Shocked the entire company."

Joe just managed not to let his eyes roll.

"They were ecstatic," Gordon continued. "You should've seen them. When we boarded that flight for Oahu, you've never seen a more pumped group of people. They're taking pictures, and they're running around like kids on Christmas morning. The celebration dinner was held on the second night and my guys were so proud of themselves. They'd never dreamed the company would honor them like this. They were bursting with pride. And then we realized that nobody from senior management was even in the room. The corporate sales support person who organized the trip goes up to the microphone and just starts handing out our coveted awards like cheap carnival prizes. It turns out that the president, executive vice president, and all of the senior vice presidents were dining elsewhere. They hadn't even bothered to show up for our celebration. We went from being somebodies to nobodies in a New York minute. All that work to turn our little part of the pyramid upside down only to have it stepped on by the upper-level elite. It was the most depressing 'celebration' of my life."

"Well, good luck to you, Gordon." Joe raised his glass. "Sounds like you're superman, so managing ALMR should be no problem for a pro like you." *Can't even fail in his own story about failure.* Tears stung the back of Joe's eyes. If there had been even a shred of hope left in his soul that Gordon wouldn't be everything the Board cracked him up to be, it shriveled up within him.

"To you, too, Joe, may this week bring you more than a pile of empty promises."

There was a long pause as Gordon let silence fall between them. Joe certainly wasn't making this easy. Charlie sure had his work cut out for him. Still Gordon was intrigued to see what he would come up with.

"Joe?"

"Huh?"

"I really am sorry that you didn't get the promotion you wanted."

"Yeah well, maybe next time. You were a perfect choice. The board did their due diligence," Joe didn't even try to mask his insincerity.

"I think we're supposed to be meeting the others in the lobby right about now," said Gordon. Joe threw down the rest of his drink, washing away the bitter memories.

PART THREE

Sessions

CHAPTER 9

It's No Secret

Tuesday–8:59 AM

Gwen surveyed the large conference room. *This place looked a lot smaller yesterday.* She took a deep breath and smoothed her skirt. In thirty seconds, they would realize what she already knew. She was in way over her head. "Good morning," Gwen leaned into the microphone. "Can you hear me?" A rumble of affirmation arose from the assembled crowd. "My name is Gwen Kelly and I am the director of sales for Advanced Biomolecular Pharmaceuticals. I want to welcome you all here this week. It is sure to be a memorable event. In our industry, it's really quite an accomplishment to be moving forward with this type of partnership, and I'd like to thank the visionaries who believe we will succeed." A tentative applause trickled forward. *They're not buying this at all,* she thought. *I wouldn't either if I was in their shoes. A partnership with our sales division is hardly a match made in heaven.*

Joe glowered at her from the back corner of the room. *Some partnership*, he thought. *I'm the damn sales vice president for my company. So why's she up there when I'm down here? It's just Gordon's way of keeping me down.* "You've got this week to pull it together, Joe," Gordon had said. "Then we're going to need to talk about the future." What was the point in talking? Why couldn't Gordon just get some guts? *Just fire me*, thought Joe. Then they'd see some action. *I carry the critical accounts in this company. I'm the one who built our cozy relationship with the FDA. You think those things will stick around if I'm gone? Not a chance.*

"We've put together quite an experience for you," Gwen continued. "In addition to our joint sessions, we'll be combining individuals from both organizations into breakout sessions to encourage cross-company team interactions. The theme for the week is leadership. In each session, we'll be examining different aspects of leadership from a variety of different perspectives. Although we come from different organizations, I'm sure that we can all agree that leadership is what we need to set and achieve our goals." *Or maybe it's what you need, Gwen*, she thought.

"With that in mind, it is my great pleasure to introduce to you our keynote speaker, Ms. Abby Bancroft, the CEO of Perfect Leadership Consulting. Abby's background runs the gamut from sales at every level to publishing. She has been involved in the training business for about fifteen years now and has worked with companies in the pharmaceutical world as well as technology, health care, and finance, to name a few. We have asked Abby to help us focus this week on our leadership theme by giving us a quick refresher on what it means to be a true leader. Ladies and gentlemen, Abby Bancroft." Applause broke out as Abby strode across the stage and grasped Gwen's hand.

"Thank you, Gwen. And thank you, ladies and gentlemen, for welcoming me here today. It is my great pleasure to introduce you to some techniques that will give you a more fulfilling and balanced life. Anyone up for that?" Laughter rippled through the audience.

"To do that, I want to share my thoughts about the line we waver on each and every day. Do you ever wake up in the morning and wonder if today is the day?" Abby paused. "If today is the day you'll be found out? If today is the day someone will discover you are an imposter and will rat you out?" All over the audience people shifted in their seats, heads began to nod. People who'd been immersed in their own thoughts snapped to attention.

"But here's the joke, and it's on all of us. No one really knows what they're doing. We are all practicing every day. The truth is, it's all a balancing act between what you believe and how you behave. Every day, you are presented with circumstances that force you to choose whether to fail or succeed. Should you just do as you're told, or should you challenge the situation in front of you? How and when should we pick our battles?"

Battles. That word resonated with Gwen. Her entire life felt like a battle right now: battling at work trying to rally the sales team; battling at home, giving whatever she had left at the end of the day; battling over whether or not to accept another job.

Jodi Eastridge, the headhunter, had called back and asked if she was available to interview this week. This was the last thing Gwen had expected. Then Jodi told her the CEO was in Tucson that week and wanted to do a "meet and greet" with her, since coincidentally Gwen was in Tucson as well. She wouldn't have to make a decision right away, though, Jodi assured her, and it was this that prompted her to agree to the meeting.

She forced herself to focus on Abby's speech. "Your words can reveal things you never thought anyone could see. They reveal your courage, your commitment, and your ability to lead. Or the opposite. How do you want your coworkers and family to talk about you? 'She was the best.' Or, 'She was a tyrant. Everything I know about leadership is contrary to her behavior.' These conversations are up for grabs and what they sound like is your choice. Can you look people in the eye and honestly say you're living an authentic life of integrity, or are you just modeling the art of sucking up? Over the next two days, in your breakout sessions, we will be walking you through some ideas and activities that will help you make sure you're on the succeeding side. One of the most important elements determining whether you fail or succeed is a passionate focus. Creating a passionate focus for yourself . . . your life . . . is crucial."

Abby paused and gazed across the crowd. Were they feeling it? "How many of you have a passionate focus in your life?" Half a dozen people raised their hands. "Typical. Only a few hands—and those raised are only flying at half mast." Laughter broke the tentative silence. *They're starting to loosen up.* "And most of you in this room have probably gone to one or a hundred workshops or seminars in your career that were supposed to fix you, right?" More laughter.

Joe snorted from his seat in the back. Who did this Abby chick think she was? Just another egotistical speaker with a multi-step plan for changing the world. *What a joke.* What was Gordon hoping to accomplish by making him listen to this kind of rah-rah crap anyway? It felt like another trap, a 'straighten up or hit the road, Jack' scenario. *Yeah,* thought Joe, *well, two can play that game, and I usually come out on top.* He crossed his arms and closed his eyes. Still blurry from last night's drinks, he tuned Abby out and went to work on his strategy.

"Let me share a story about a friend of mine," said Abby. "Many years ago, toward the end of his last foray into corporate 'bigwigdom,' he attended a seminar about personal responsibility. As people gathered that morning, they mingled and sipped coffee and munched on the breakfast goodies, just like you did today. Some people, who were obviously veterans of these types of events, were introducing themselves to each other and asking the usual 'what do you do' types of questions, trying to determine their rank in the group. Others, feeling like complete nobodies, remained on the silent sidelines as if this were a pre-teen dance. But one person stood out to my friend. He was a very large and unkempt young man named George. George was an electrical engineer and had brought a prototype of the newest handheld gadget with him. George glowed as he shared his device. He was talkative, articulate, and flowing with joy. When it was time to get started, the group facilitator seated everyone in a circle and asked them to introduce themselves, and share a story that was personal or life affirming. As they sat, my friend watched something strange take place. George was sinking deeper and deeper into his seat . . . curling up into a ball as if trying to melt into the leather. When it was time for George to introduce himself, the confident gadget-wielding guy of a few moments ago had vanished, and a new George had taken his place. He whispered 'I am George . . . and the world is crushing me.'" Abby paused and looked out at the crowd. *How many people out there are like George?* she wondered.

"What George didn't realize was it wasn't the world that was crushing him—it was his attitude. He was choosing not to recognize what drove him, his passion. When he was engaged in something he was passionate about, he was upright and bold. When he allowed negative thoughts to take over, he became uptight and cold. With that in mind, I want to share with you a simple recipe that will help you change your life.

"For some of you this will be a refresher, and for others a brand new opportunity," Abby continued. "It's not a secret. We can learn to create our lives through our focused thoughts. Like George in the story, you are not a victim of circumstance or events. You are a self-determining individual. Every day you create your life through your thoughts, choices, and actions. You decide whether to cower, cope, or create. How do you greet each day? Do you wake up in the morning and as you sit there on the edge of your bed scratching your head or rubbing your eyes, decide today you will just cower or cope? Or do you use what I call 'the PH factor' and draw on your power and hope to create the life you wish to live? Ladies and gentlemen, you need to allow your focused thoughts to lead you toward a dynamic destiny. Your mind is your most valuable ally. But it can also be your most relentless adversary. By taking charge of your mind, you take charge of your life."

As she waited for the power of her message to sink in, Abby caught a glimpse of Charlie sitting toward the back of the room. She had to admit, he looked even better this morning after a shower and shave. *But now isn't the time to think about it,* she told herself. *Not now, not ever.* Taking charge of your mind, indeed! Easier said than done. . . .

"The first part of the recipe is to understand how your mind works." Abby forced herself to focus on the group before her. "It's in a constant state of activity . . . even when you sleep, your unconscious mind is still working, keeping your body alive and regenerating. And that's a good thing, right? But during our waking moments, we think one thought at a time and that thought ultimately directs our body to respond in one way or another. Your first thought in the morning might be to pull the covers over your head and hide, or to seize the day and hit the ground running. With that in mind, wouldn't you agree it seems we should put more effort into creating positive thoughts moving us in the direction we want to go? Once you know where you are and where you are going, you need to blow up the bureaucracy. You need to *Challenge the Process* both personally and professionally. You don't see successful people wandering aimlessly. Organization and balance is key. Let your thoughts grow flowers, not weeds."

She's on a roll, thought Charlie. He'd heard this speech many times before, and it never failed to amaze him that people could hear the message and still miss the point. *Keep going, Abby.*

Nail 'em with the passion talk. When people finally understood, it changed their lives.

"So my suggestion is simple. Get a piece of paper and write the following headers on it: Personal, Family, Professional, Social, Financial, and Spiritual." Abby then refreshed them in the art of goal setting. She hammered home that writing a list of specific goals for areas in their life and then targeting specific actions to accomplish them was the key.

"And don't forget to put these actions on your calendar, right along with your meetings and your due dates and your social life. Keeping things in front of you keeps them fresh. Before you know it, you will have achieved them and be on to new and loftier goals. How? By focusing your mind, your time, and your energy on what is important to you, on what is real. If you take this very primary step, the passion pilot lamp will begin to smolder.

"Unfortunately, many of you are going to stop right there. Itty-bitty bit of flame and you think you've got it covered." Abby leaned into her words, drawing people in as if revealing a mystery. "Lots of people do. The workshop is over, so you go home and put the workbook on the shelf. But keep in mind, leadership is about your journey. It is not about the goals and tasks. Those are mere milestones along the way. The journey's lessons, the learning you draw from it, that's what deepens your passion and leads to your destiny, your legacy. Passion isn't about the having; it's about the seeking. Passion shows up in your life when you focus on what you really care about. On what's real, to you. And great leaders are willing to suffer for their cause, whether it be saving lives or ensuring a healthy balance sheet.

"For a lot of you, the naysayer voice inside your head is probably spinning at light-speed right now. Grab onto that! Have you ever stopped to pay attention to what you really value? Let's give it a try.

"If you would, please take out the Values worksheet from your packet." Paper rustled throughout the room as people shuffled their notes. Gwen reached into a manila folder and pulled out the page. She must have overlooked it during the pre-work.

Abby was already walking people through it. "You'll see a list of value words at the top of the page. Take a minute or two and choose your top ten. Be sure to focus on what you really want and not on what you think would be politically correct."

Gwen stared at the list. How could she choose just ten? She skimmed over the list and circled *balance, excellence, family, health, friends, teamwork, fun, spirituality, growth,* and *financial security.*

"Got 'em?" Abby asked. "Now narrow it down to five."

Lose five? thought Gwen. It had been hard enough whittling it down to ten. She bit her bottom lip and started crossing out words until *family, health, spirituality, balance,* and *excellence* remained.

"If you've got a list of five, then there's just one more step," Abby said. "Select the number one value in your life." She could almost hear the wheels in their brains spinning. "It's tough, isn't it?" she asked. "These are tough calls to make, but the truth is, you subconsciously make these decisions every day when you decide where to focus your time and energy. The question is, are you focusing that time and energy on something you're passionate about, or not?

"So here's the big question. If the single word left on your list is the thing you're most passionate about, does that value weave its way through your everyday life? And if not, why?"

Balance. The word stared back at Gwen. It tugged at her heart. "That's it," she whispered. "That's what I really want." *To stop this tug-of-war between my family and my job. But here I am, miles from home, away from the kids, interviewing for a job that will move us to a different city because I'm failing where I am.* The conflict stirred up feelings in Gwen she'd ignored for years. *Who am I kidding?* Tears filled her eyes and escaped down her cheek.

Abby felt the energy shifting in the room. "If you're wondering how to connect to what you care deeply about, I want to give you a few tips. First, stop projecting your passion into the future. Ask yourself, *what do I love doing right now? How does it connect to what I value?* This does not need to be heroic. Don't wait until some future date to begin. Beginning brings clarity. Beginning shows commitment. Again, this is not a secret. It is the Law of Attraction and it has been known for centuries. You have created your life as it now is. If your garden has more weeds than flowers, then turn your soil and plant again. Focus on *what do I want my life to look like,* not *what do I have to do today.* This allows you to think about the end result. Your leadership choice, regardless of your position, is about your story, your legacy, and your masterpiece. Over the next two days you will hear our Five Practices of Exemplary Leaders model mentioned many times. It is about open, honest, and authentic communication. Leadership is not a series of costume changes, folks. It is about the real you in real time . . . real life. It is personal and, yes, it is a choice. Wherever you are in your life . . . it is time to make the choice.

"And finally, your leadership action should include ending the abusive use of power to exploit others. It's time to take back your life. And urge others to take back theirs. It's time to make one choice . . . *leadership*. It's time to join an integrity revolution, the personal revolt against those who want to make it a decision between integrity and mortgage. Never fear the challenge, ladies and gentlemen, never back away. When we finally understand what really matters to us, that's when we show up as a beacon for others, speak up to inequities and insults, step up to challenge the mundane or mediocre, and serve others with a sense of gratitude without being subservient. Most importantly, it is in this valiant effort that we create our own life legacy. Our masterpiece. Ladies and gentlemen, it's about one choice. It's about time. Thank you."

Applause filled the room. Abby grinned. She loved to see people connect. "Thank you, ladies and gentlemen, for your time and attention," she said. "Before you head into your first breakout session, I want to introduce my colleague, who will be working with some of you over the next few days. Charlie, could you please stand up so everyone can see you?"

Charlie stood and gave the audience a cocky wave. He caught Abby's eye and smiled, holding her gaze a few beats longer than necessary. She smiled back, or smirked, he couldn't tell.

"Charlie Verona will be sharing his secret recipes of leadership. He'll be here most of the week, walking you through what we've covered this morning, and taking those of you who wish down a deeper path. In other words, he'll help you really turn up the magnificence in your life.

"Thank you again," Abby added. "I will be around for the rest of the workshops, popping in and out of your sessions. If you have any questions, please don't hesitate to take me aside. I would love to hear your stories."

I'll tell you my story, thought Joe. *It's a story about how a new CEO completely ignores his existing talent and makes them come to sessions like this.* He needed a drink. Too early. He'd have to settle for a smoke instead.

CHAPTER 10

A Grenade for Your Thoughts

Tuesday–10:04 AM

Abby worked her way toward the refreshment table and poured herself a cup of coffee, her third. It had been a long night. The massage at the spa should have relaxed her, but Charlie kept creeping into her mind, and she figured it must've been seeing him for the first time in two months. She'd called Dennis before going to bed, but had gotten his voice mail and hung up without leaving a message.

Charlie, minus his leather jacket, was at the front of the room writing on a flip chart. Today he was wearing a black silk shirt and jeans, loafers, no socks. *What is it with this guy*, she thought, realizing he exuded a casual attractiveness that made her knees wobbly. *Well, you're not exactly one to talk.* Her thirty-minute debate over which outfit best accentuated her figure had been shamelessly for his benefit, even though she was loath to admit it. She caught Charlie's eye and grinned.

"Good morning, Charlie."

"Abby! Great to see you. Nice keynote. You really set the tone."

"Thanks," she replied. "I thought I would hang with you this morning. Have you had a chance to meet Joe Vanderson yet?"

"Haven't been that lucky." Charlie shifted his attention back to the flip chart. *Going to be tough to stay on track with Abby in the room,* he thought.

Joe, alone outside, stubbed out his cigarette and exhaled. He'd managed to tune out most of Abby's speech. Judging by the thunderous applause at the end, the rest of the crowd had eaten it up. *What a bunch of sheep.* He checked his watch. *Six more hours of this garbage before dinner.* And the breakout sessions with Mr. "Tough Guy" Verona up next. *Hmmm, that Abby practically blushed at the mention of his name. I wonder if they've got something going on the side. Not a bad setting for a little romantic pick-me-up,* thought Joe as he headed back indoors. He wished he'd paid more attention to the signs. *Where is the damn meeting room, anyway?*

"Good morning," said Gordon, encouraging the last of the stragglers to find their seats. Joe stormed the room as if going into battle, then sank noisily into a seat in the back. "Let's take our seats and get started. I'd like to introduce Charlie Verona. Charlie has been delivering real-world leadership from the inside out for nearly twelve years and has been working with individuals and organizations in the U.S. and abroad to help them clarify their core principles and beliefs and develop their leadership ability. His reputation assures me that we're in for a wild ride over the next two days. But, knowing the quality and reputation of PLC, I know we're in good hands. So let's keep an open mind and trust the process."

"Thank you, Gordon." Charlie accepted Gordon's warm handshake and turned to the group. "Ladies and gentlemen, for the next couple of days we are going to submerge ourselves in a conversation about leadership. Leadership is about open, honest, and authentic communication and the deep relationships created from that behavior. As a leader, you need to show up in an open, honest, and authentic way no matter who you're with or what the circumstances. Why? Because those who choose to join you deserve nothing less. And in order to carry out that style of communication, you have to build an organization of transparency and trust." He leaned against the table and shifted modes.

"When you're on your morning commute, do you ever *really* look at other drivers? Whenever I'm on the freeway, I look at people in their cars, and most of them look like they're sleep-driving zombies. They have this 'bored with life' glaze over their eyes. Reminds me of Haley Joel Osment in *The Sixth Sense.* 'I see dead people,'" Charlie whispered. Heads nodded in agreement.

"And then there are the people who are reaching into the glove compartment to grab their work mask, the one that covers up their insecurity and shows people they're in complete control of the situation. And then on the way home they take off the work mask and slap on the mommy or daddy mask.

"It seems to me corporate America is churning out and burning out managers instead of leaders. It's creating thousands of morally and ethically challenged automatons instead of people who really care about others and the work they do. And you know what, I'm not really surprised." Charlie pushed off from the rostrum and began to walk between the strategically placed tables.

"In grade school they drill students on facts and figures, but character and interpersonal skills? Let kids develop those in the rough-and-tumble of recess—where more often than not, might makes right. In business schools they spend an inordinate amount of time teaching you everything you'd ever want to know about managing systems, policies, and procedures, and then throw in a tiny amount of effort, if any, on what real leadership truly is. And when you finally enter the corporate jungle, if you have that management 'spark,' they send you to 'supervisor training' where they drill and grill you on how to control, get results from, and discipline the laggards. And then, when you've worked your way up the ladder, right when you're ready to retire, they send you to a leadership class where they tell you that you should have done it better all this time. Does this experience resonate with anyone in this room?" Several people raised their hands. "Well I'm here to change all that." Charlie grinned; he was just getting started.

"Sometimes we compare ourselves to the likes of Nelson Mandela, Gandhi, Martin Luther King Jr., or Lincoln. And of course we seem to come up short. Well, that doesn't matter. At some time or another, you've likely had a leadership role thrust upon you, and you've risen to the challenge—at the PTA, in your family, in the community. Whenever you are in the position to influence a process, you have an opportunity to lead those who choose to join with you. But those who join willingly will only be those who trust you. A trusted leader ignites others to action. But you won't ignite anyone if you aren't clear about your own beliefs. Without personal passion, you have zero hope of creating the kind of bonds that inspire others. Clarifying that passion will be at the heart of our conversation over the next two days. If you remember nothing else out of these sessions, remember this: to connect with your ability to lead, you must first connect deeply with yourself."

Joe shifted in his seat. Charlie was already hitting too close to home. If he'd wanted therapy, he would have gone to a shrink like Nora had asked. Now this guy wanted him to explore his feelings? *No thank you.* Joe shuddered. *Trust and transparency, nice platitudes, but the real world says you've got to work with who you've got, whether they trust you or not.* If this guy was going to harp on relationships all day, then Gordon was just wasting his money. He'd never let anyone get that close. If they ever got a look inside—well, they weren't going to.

Charlie pressed on. "Our conversations will refresh you in the leadership basics and bring you new insights on how to lead in today's corporate culture. This is more of an interactive conversation than an academic process. I like to toss what I call 'thought grenades' out on the table. For each of you, they might go off at that moment, or in the days or months to come. But they *will* explode." Charlie scanned the room, checking eyeballs, as he waited for the impact of his words to settle across the audience.

"Before you came this week, we asked you to do some pre-work. Go ahead and pull that out. We asked you to take a moment and reflect on a time when you believed you were at your best as a leader in any aspect of your life. We asked you to think about that situation and jot some notes for discussion about what happened. What needed to be done? Who was there to help? How did you overcome the odds? Now at your tables, I want each of you to share your story. When you're all finished we will examine the common themes."

As the hum of conversation filled the room, Charlie wandered from table to table, keeping a close eye on Joe. Would he participate? Would it be a real effort? Judging by his body language and that of the group he'd wound up with, things didn't look promising. As the groups wrapped up their conversations, Charlie brought their focus back to the center of the room.

"What words showed up at your tables? Let's start over here and I'll keep track on the flip chart."

Within a few minutes, a number of duplicated words filled the page. "You can see from the pattern developing here that different personal best experiences share common themes. If you are going to be the leader, these thoughts, patterns, and behaviors need to become common practice for you. So what does this tell us?" Charlie asked rhetorically.

"The behavior of a leader is a reflection of his or her values. Our premise is simple. Leadership is the art of mobilizing others to want to struggle for shared aspirations. It is a choice about creating open, honest, and authentic relationships that urge others to want to discover their own power and focus on what matters to them and their community."

If that's leadership, then I'm the King of Fantasy Land, muttered Joe. *I'm not going to drag anyone through my past or my childhood just to make them follow me. Charlie certainly does enjoy his psychobabble.* He glanced at his workbook and slashed an X through the part about leadership being a courageous choice. *Choose, my foot,* he said to himself. *I didn't get a choice.* Charlie was still talking. *What an arrogant bastard. Just crowing to hear himself crow.*

"As I mentioned earlier, most people who consider themselves leaders are actually acting like managers. Management is usually defined in terms of getting stuff done; process, structure, control, and planning. Leadership, meanwhile, is usually defined as inspiring, encouraging, challenging, and growing people.

"If I asked you how you want to be remembered, would you say 'Gee Charlie, I'd like people to remember me as the person who always promptly returned e-mail.'" Laughter rippled through the room. "Of course not. People want to be remembered for the positive impact they had on other people. That's why leadership must be at the core of your organization, and not hovering somewhere around the edges like so many management models prescribe. It's the transformational leaders who are making the positive change in our world. They understand that to get the productivity they desire, they need to inspire those around them to want to participate. They understand management is about things, but leadership, leadership is about people. Leadership is how you get management done. So, if you want to transform yourself or your workplace, today is as good a day as any to get started. Become a leader by focusing on the people and allowing the right activities to fall into place. Our model is simple. We offer Five Practices of Exemplary Leaders to keep on your true path. Let me share some slides:

"Your credibility matters so . . . *Model the Way*. How? Clarify values by finding your voice and affirming shared ideals. Set the example by aligning actions with shared values.

"Your voice matters so . . . *Inspire a Shared Vision*. How? Envision the future by imagining exciting and ennobling possibilities. Enlist others in a common vision by appealing to shared aspirations.

"Your action matters so . . . *Challenge the Process*. How? Search for opportunities by seizing the initiative and by looking outward for innovative ways to improve. Experiment and take risks by constantly generating small wins and learning from experience.

"Your gift matters so . . . *Enable Others to Act*. How? Foster collaboration by building trust and facilitating relationships. Strengthen others by increasing self-determination and developing competence.

"Your gratitude matters so . . . *Encourage the Heart*. How? Recognize contributions by showing appreciation for individual excellence. Celebrate the values and victories by creating a spirit of community.

"But don't just define leadership. Design it into your own life and then live by design, not by default. The days for executives to dispense answers from the top of Management Mountain are over, my friends. Leaders offer questions, not answers. Today's workplace is constantly changing and all the people in it should consider themselves learners first and foremost. Many of the young people coming into the workplace today are smarter, brighter, and more fearless than any generation before them. They want to participate now, not fifteen or twenty years from now. Tune in to that enthusiasm with dignity. When I first joined the workforce, the times and the organizational culture told me to sit down and shut up . . . the powers that be would get back to me when they thought I had something worthwhile to say. Great leadership takes the exact opposite approach." He scanned the room, catching as many people's eyes as possible. "Great leadership begins in this room, today." The room erupted with applause. Charlie beamed.

Within a few minutes, armed with fresh coffee, Charlie had them split into groups of four or five, sharing obstacles they would like to challenge. He wandered through the room, sitting in each group for a few minutes, encouraging them to dig deeper.

Joe watched him out of the corner of his eye. *What an arrogant blowhard.* Still, Joe knew how to work the group. He could fake it for a few more minutes.

"What about you, Joe?" Charlie asked, hovering over their group. "Who are you and what do you want?"

"Everything you've said sounds pretty good to me," Joe cocked his head and stared at Charlie. "I don't think I really have all that much to add."

"I'm not talking about me. I know who I am and what I want. I want to know about you."

So he was going to push harder than the others. *Fine,* Joe thought. *I'll push back.* "I want to be successful even under difficult real-life constraints such as time pressure, high risk, and personal responsibility amid shifting conditions," he said with a smirk. *What do you think now, Mr. Tough Guy? What does your leadership system say about that?*

Charlie worked the conversation like a matador. Encouraging Joe to charge honestly ahead, he swirled the conversation around like a cape. He'd revived many a man like Joe over the years; guys who could talk the talk but couldn't walk the walk.

He called for a break, giving everyone a few minutes to stretch their legs. Joe took the bait and pulled Charlie aside.

"Look," said Joe, staring right through Charlie. "I don't know who you think you are, but I'm not happy with what's going on in here. People have a right to their privacy, and some of your comments border on harassment and intimidation."

"I'm not sure what you are getting at, Joe," Charlie replied. "We've only just begun."

"Who are you to second-guess the decisions made by others?" Joe shot back. "You don't know me. You don't work at my company. If I took your tone back to my team, they'd hang me from the rafters."

"Joe, let's take a step back. Why don't you get some fresh air and then give the rest of the morning a chance. I think you'll see things from a different perspective by the end of the day. Gordon asked you to trust the process, and I think that's good advice."

"I don't care what you think. In a few days, you'll be gone and I'll be left with a whole bunch of coworkers who want to learn and grow instead of work." Joe turned on his heel and headed for the door.

Abby hightailed it over to Charlie. "Everything OK?"

"Just ducky. That guy's a piece of work, but nothing I can't handle. Still, it's not going to be an easy day. I've already seen his LPI scores and he's not going to be happy with them."

"That bad, huh?"

"About the worst I've ever seen. Still, it might be the kind of shock he needs to get back on track. Maybe it's none of my business, but why is Gordon so interested in keeping that guy on the team? Does he have pictures of Gordon playing golf with Satan?"

Abby snickered. "Not exactly. But he does manage their top clients and is tight with their primary venture capitalists. There was some bad blood in that area when he wasn't selected as CEO. If he left altogether, the money might follow."

Joe paced back and forth outside the conference room. He didn't know how much more he could handle. Still, he was curious about the leadership inventory thing. Surely someone would realize his potential and score him off the charts? That would be enough ammunition to get Charlie off his back; Gordon too for that matter. When he returned to his seat, Charlie was walking people through the four stages of grief. What a melodramatic idiot. Like people were going to get all worked up over a survey.

"Sometimes we find that when people read their Leadership Practices Inventory for the first time, it's pretty rough," explained Charlie. "So let me introduce you to SARA." He grabbed a marker and headed back to the flip chart. "That's not a woman, unfortunately, but an acronym. And SARA can help you work through your feelings when you first open your LPI and see your results. At first, you may be shocked. Then, you will likely experience some anger. This is black-and-white truth on the page, and that can be hard to swallow at first. But soon, you'll move into recognition and finally acceptance. From that point, we can really work with you to improve. So, go ahead and open your envelopes. Take a few minutes to process the information, and then we'll open up the floor for a group discussion and questions."

Joe ripped into his envelope and froze. He wasn't going to make it past shock. His temples throbbed and blood rushed to his head. His heart pounded as if he was going to explode. He looked wildly for the door and bolted like a jackrabbit. Charlie moved to follow but Gordon cut him off at the door. "I've got this one, Charlie."

"Joe, wait!" Gordon ran after his sprinting colleague. "Let's talk about this."

"Talk?" Joe yelled. "You want to talk after attacking me on this, this *thing*? Who the hell do you think you are? Why would I ever want to talk to you again?"

"It's not an attack, Joe. It's the truth. This survey asked us to honestly evaluate the frequency of your leadership behavior and this is what we see."

"I don't care how you phrase it. Put a bow on it for all I care. It's pretty obvious you want me out. But did you have to humiliate me like this in front of everyone? That was cheap, and to be honest, I didn't think you'd sink that low."

Joe choked back a sob and stormed toward the front door. There was nowhere to go. Without thinking or really paying attention to where he was going, he boarded a tour bus parked outside the entrance, took three or four lunges to the rear, and crumpled into the corner in a heap, oblivious to the startled looks of the other passengers. He didn't care where the bus was going as long as it took him far, far away from Gordon, Charlie, and his bullshit 360-degree review process. Nothing mattered now except being alone.

The meeting room crackled with tension. "Let's take another quick break," said Charlie. "Some people have very strong reactions when they only see the negative in their scores. I think we need to have a few minutes to redirect our energy in a more positive direction."

Gordon and Abby converged on Charlie. "What do we do now?" Abby asked.

"Yeah. How far do you want us to go with this?" Gordon was clearly upset.

"I haven't seen a reaction like that in quite a while. I've seen people get upset, but I've never had anyone cut and run before." Charlie was embarrassed. He'd never had so little control over a session. "Do you think he's coming back?"

"Unlikely," Gordon replied.

"I've got to get this session and these folks back on track. Can we discuss this over dinner?"

"Good idea," Abby nodded—in retrospect, she thought, perhaps a little too eagerly. "I'll make reservations."

CHAPTER 11

The Perfect Fall
Tuesday–10:47 AM

The tour coach driver returned from the office and settled down at the wheel. Joe felt the bus roar to life and made no move to get off. He didn't care. He'd rather be anywhere than at some ridiculous meeting getting his managerial techniques incorrectly evaluated by some arrogant twit. No one asked for a ticket or asked him to leave. He squinted against the late morning glare from the sun, rubbing his temples, seething with anger. Gordon had won. He'd wanted him out and he'd stopped at nothing to get the job done. It had all been a sham. The offsite, the dinner at Jake's, the team building, it was all just a ruse to keep him off track while they plastered him in the survey. He hadn't even seen it coming. *After all I've given to the company. My time, my talent, hell, I even sacrificed my marriage. And that was it.*

The bus rolled along the scorching highway, soaking up the desert sun. Half a dozen tourists from the hotel were on board on their way to some sort of outing. They chatted giddily among themselves, unaware of the turmoil going on in the head of the latest passenger to join their trip. Saguaro cacti slipped by the window waving at the world with outstretched arms. A wildcat bounded alongside the bus. Where the hell were they going?

A moment of awareness came over Joe, who felt compelled to at least find out what their destination was. "Where are we going?" Joe moved forward, asking the woman sitting at the back of the group.

"Colossal Caves," she replied, pulling a brochure from her purse.

Colossal Caves, thought Joe. *You've got to be kidding. Well . . . whatever, as long as it isn't at that damn seminar.*

The ride was long and Joe hated long road trips. After what seemed an eternity, the bus driver tapped on the microphone. "Welcome to Colossal Caves, which is on the National Register of Historic Places. This cave was used for centuries by prehistoric peoples before it was 'discovered' in 1879. Since that time, it has been an object of interest and attention for everyone from train robbers to a University of Arizona president . . . " The driver's voice trailed off into the distance as his rehearsed monologue fell on Joe's deaf ears. Joe's thoughts instead turned to his loneliness and how he had lost the love of all those close to him. His wife, who'd once always accompanied him to these meetings, could no longer put up with him. Even his niece and nephew no longer spoke to him.

The bus pulled through a gate and into a parking lot. Memories came back to him of how he and Nora had taken Lindy and Bobby to things like this when the kids were little, when they were pretending to be a family. *Nora tried too hard sometimes to be their mother. . . .*

"We're here, so gather your things and meet up outside the bus." The driver eased the bus into a dusty slot. "We need to go over some safety issues before we head out for the day."

Yeah, right, thought Joe. *That's what I need, someone else to tell me what to do. I'm a grown man for crying out loud.* Joe decided to ditch the group and head in the opposite direction. If he was going to be stuck out here, he was at least going to do what he chose to do on his own terms.

He followed a sign saying "Ladder Tour." Although he didn't know what that meant, he knew it was the opposite direction to where all these camera-toting, rubbernecking gapers were going to be.

He spotted a table of lanterns just inside the cave entrance. Joe grabbed a lantern and turned the switch on the base. It lit and shed light down the steep slope into the dark cave. He was still furious, but at least this Boy Scout adventure kept him distracted. *I'll just sneak down here a ways and have a few cigarettes by myself. Who needs those know-it-alls back at the seminar?*

Joe walked down some seriously tight paths weaving past evil-looking rock formations. The shapes felt like they were glaring down on him, judging him as he had been judged back at the hotel. He felt small and insignificant, yet at the same time the cave was eerily beautiful. *Like a church,* thought Joe. The stillness, the scent, the dim glow of the lantern. It swept him back to childhood times. He saw the sanctuary, the altar, the fiery preacher damning them all to hell if they didn't repent. He found a low rock and sat, allowing the religious feeling to wash over him.

Joe lit up another cigarette and watched the smoke circle up through the stillness and be trapped on the roof of the cave. He thought about the events that had transpired earlier that day. About the assault he had faced and how he had been taken for a fool by Gordon and the rest saying this seminar was designed to "help" him. His feelings of loneliness started to drift back. He felt comfortable here though, in his own cocoon.

Joe noticed the light on his lantern start to flicker. He picked up his lantern and shook it. *Hmmm, battery running out,* he thought. He became concerned about what it would mean to be hundreds of feet below the surface of the earth with no light. At that, the lantern dimmed and left Joe with only the red embers at the end of his cigarette giving any light.

It was the blackest black Joe had ever felt, as if all hope and light had been sucked from the earth. As if mankind had ceased to exist. Fear gripped his soul. He reached for a wall, a railing, anything to steady his pounding heart. But there was only space. He lunged forward, grabbing for a rock he had remembered jutting out from the wall beside him, but he couldn't find it.

Joe reached for his cigarette lighter and could feel his hands shaking uncontrollably as the gravity of his situation became apparent. He flicked two or three times and a glow of light gave him a brief hint as to his surroundings. In his panic, as he turned, his thumb slipped and the flame scorched his finger. He dropped the lighter and heard it thump across the floor of the cave.

Joe fell to his knees and searched wildly in the inky blackness. His hands patted the floor, looking for his only source of light. Joe crawled around for what seemed an eternity, feeling this way and that, crawling forward and backward.

His feet and knees scraped around the floor until suddenly, behind him, his feet reached to emptiness, nothing, just more empty black. As Joe gasped and lurched with surprise, his knees also began to slip. His fingers reached out in a last-chance effort to save himself, but it was too late. He slid backward uncontrollably down the ledge.

Joe struggled to catch the breath that was jerking through his chest in wild patterns. Where was he? How far had he fallen? He couldn't breathe. He couldn't yell. They'd never miss him. Nobody even knew where he was. He didn't exist.

CHAPTER 12

Practice Makes Perfect
Tuesday—10:06 AM

Gwen grabbed a doughnut and headed for the meeting room. *I wish there was more time between sessions,* she thought. The word *family* was still seared on her mind. She hadn't even had time to check in with them yet today. Is that what corporate leadership was going to be like? Always running from point A to point B? Maybe she could fit in a quick call before Sam's breakout session. She pulled her cell phone out of her purse. Low signal. Changing directions, Gwen headed toward the pool patio. The bars on her phone leapt to life. A message.

"Gwen, it's Jodi from Eastridge Executive Recruitment. I've got you all set up for the interview on Wednesday. It's with Gordon Murphy of ALMR. He's at the same hotel as you in Tucson. Is that a coincidence or what? He wants to get together at 5:15 on Wednesday evening. You're supposed to meet him in the lobby and, shoot, I forgot to ask what he looks like. I'll have to call you back." *Unbelievable.* The interview was with Gordon Murphy? The same Gordon who ran the company that was partnering with ABP. Did Jodi realize how awkward this was going to be? *I haven't even told Jerry I'm looking. . . .*

Gwen flicked the phone shut and glanced at the time display. Two minutes late. At least they couldn't start without her. Or maybe they would. *This change might be what I need,* she thought. *Stock up on leadership stuff at this offsite and then start fresh with a new company.* She'd met Gordon at the keynote session. Seemed like an upstanding guy, and who wouldn't want to live in San Diego?

Sam placed his briefcase on the front table and surveyed the Indigo Room.

"You sure you're up for this, old man?" Abby asked, grinning at Sam.

"Oh, you bet. It's just like riding a bike."

"Thanks for stepping in like this, Sam—I really appreciate it."

"No problem. I'm really proud of you and Charlie. You've both come a long way since I took your sorry little brains under my wing. Now let's get this show on the road shall we? You want to do the intros?"

Abby turned to the room. "All right, folks, we've made these sessions fairly small so that we'll have time for real conversation. So grab a chair and we'll get started. First, I want to introduce Sam Arthur. Sam was my mentor earlier in my career.

In fact, I owe a great deal to him. He has worked in the real world and taught the leadership principles you are about to hear to thousands of people. Sam, why don't you take it away?"

Sam rubbed his hands together and grinned. "All right, team. We need to peel the artichoke, so to speak. It's time to open up a bit." Sam stared at them for what seemed like an eternity, creating a new more serious environment, and then led off with his opening statement.

"Leadership is the art of mobilizing others to want to struggle for shared aspirations. It's about the questions—not the answers," Sam began. "So, let me ask you a question right off the bat. If your team isn't following, what do you do?"

"Replace 'em!" shot a voice from the back of the room.

"Oh yes, sometimes that would be nice!" chuckled Sam. "I've dealt with a few humdingers in my day. But letting people go, even constantly telling them what to do, that's an outdated model. That's the way the world worked when I was coming up through the ranks. There weren't tools for leadership evaluation like you have today. And we walked to school uphill both ways, barefoot in the snow, fighting off bears with our notebooks," Sam said with a wink. "No, the answer is to become a better leader by weaving The Five Practices of Exemplary Leadership into your life."

Sam scrawled the five phrases across the flip chart at the front of the room. "If you're not present, you can't lead, so let's start with *Model the Way*. What does that mean?"

"Being there?" asked a woman in the front row.

"In what way? Is it just clocking in and clocking out? Or is it something more?"

"I guess it would be more. Paying attention. Caring about things . . ."

"That's right. If you don't show up, you're going to lose credibility, and credibility matters. You need to blaze a credibility trail for others to follow. People join with others who are honest, competent, inspiring, and forward looking. That's what our research has proven time and time again. So, be clear on your own key values, beliefs, and principles—and be willing to share them. And lead by example: take important stands on important issues and act in ways that are consistent with your stated values.

"Next you need to speak up by *Inspiring a Shared Vision,* because your voice matters. I like to do this through stories that connect to the heart, not just facts or figures. Don't get me wrong, we all need the detail, but your passion needs to be part of a bigger picture. Do you think that Martin Luther King Jr. could have rallied a nation if he'd said 'I have ten measurable objectives' instead of 'I have a dream'? Leaders share their dreams, folks. They breathe life into their visions and communicate clearly for understanding. Nobody wants to be handled like pawns in a chess game. Provide the direction, but give people the choice to make their own moves.

"Your leadership vision should not be about B.S.—it should be about P.S., passionate stories. That's what drives people to bring their full selves to the task. People at work can get lost in a fog. They need a master map and a real sense of clear, open roads," Sam continued. "When visions fade or don't exist, people grip the wheel a little tighter . . . they turn down the tunes . . . they let go of their loved ones . . . they aren't having fun.

Productivity screeches to a halt. And the leader is to blame. Why? It is the job of the leader to create a clear map. Weave passion and direction into all that you do and your vision will become the map of choice. Joiners will join. Fence-sitters will climb down on your side of the line, and eventually even some of the die-hards will start to shift toward you. People will jump at the chance to give their input. They will be inspired. And when you reach that point, success lies just ahead."

Sam paused a moment to let his message sink in. He surveyed the room, enjoying the nods of agreement and understanding that he saw. *They're getting the message,* he thought.

"And you must step up by *Challenging the Process,* because your actions matter. Experiment, take risks. Be sure everyone learns from their mistakes and their successes too. I once took over a division of a company that was totally paralyzed. The old division head was a total control freak. He'd even had his receptionist and accounting supervisor spend an hour a day being human time clocks. It was absurd. Once I uncovered this nonsense, I confronted it head on.

"The situation was ridiculous, and yet it was a great learning moment. I asked both of them to join me in the middle of the main floor. Waving the time sheet binder over my head, I grabbed the attention of all eighty or so employees in the room. I told the entire story and said, 'This is a stupid thing to do, and you are not stupid!' Then I dropped the binder into a wastebasket with a thunderous bang. At first, they were all stunned, and then whistling and cheering broke out across the room. People suddenly understood what it meant to challenge. To take risks. They started searching for and stopping the stupid things getting in their way each day. It was like taking a pebble out of their shoe. Everything began to feel better.

"Wastebasket revelry is a daily exercise for real leaders. Your action matters. Relish the opportunity to prove it can be done. Help others see obstacles as challenges for growth, not barriers. And in everything you do, stand for integrity. Because it's not the fact that you're standing that matters, it's where you're standing."

"And speaking of standing," Abby cut in, "let's take a quick break. We'll get started again in ten minutes."

During the break, Abby sidled up to Gwen, who seemed to be a little distracted about something. "You doing OK this morning, Gwen?" she asked.

"Oh, hi, Abby," Gwen said with a sigh. "I'm just taking it all in. I can see why all of you love Sam so much. I'm learning a lot."

"Good. It was a great idea—asking him to share with the group today. I guess I could say you're stepping up."

Gwen laughed a little nervously.

"I know I hardly know you," Abby said, "but I'm proud of you. I know your team's been struggling, but you really have a chance to turn it all around. I think once you really understand the idea of leadership, you're going to be outstanding."

"Thanks, Abby. It means a lot that you'd say that. I guess I just have to start believing in myself."

"We've saved the best for last," said Sam as the group filtered back into the room. "Leadership isn't about being served, although some of you probably wish it was. Nope, it's about serving others, allowing innovation to flourish and coaching the best out of your team. It shows them that their growth is important to you and to their fellows.

"So if we are showing up, speaking up, and stepping up, how should we help others grow? By serving up our time and effort while using our fourth and fifth practices. The fourth is *Enable Others to Act* and the final practice is *Encourage the Heart.*

"Now, enabling others is more than just delegating. It's about developing confidence and competence in others. You need to give folks more control over their work. For some of us it's not easy letting go. But to develop your leadership credibility you must begin to share information more deeply. You've got to leave room for discretion on decisions and blow up the rules to the best of your ability.

"As people take on more and more responsibility, the leader pays attention and lets everyone know it. How? By creating a variety of ways to say thank you. It's amazing how even small praise can ignite someone to great achievements. One of the best ways I know to say thank you is the underestimated little personal, handwritten thank-you note. Today e-mail praise is too easy and too overdone. Meaningful, specific notes are the way to go. If you've ever received one, you probably still have it. Notes like that are usually kept for a lifetime. Delivering them is the key. You need to make that personal as well. I have found sending them through snail mail is best. And if you really want to make an impact, send the note to someone in your team member's family. Nothing is more powerful in my book.

"As you heard from Abby during the kickoff, leadership requires commitment. That's why I look at The Five Practices as a Commitment Circle. You can't be an exemplary leader practicing only one . . . you must learn to allow each of them to feed into the others.

"And the best way to do that is by using your LPI scores to guide you. You must take a hard look and see where you need work. Then create a plan. Plan to share your vision and values with your team; share your LPI scores to get more detailed feedback, and embrace the fact that leadership is not about business, it's very personal."

"That wraps up our session for this morning," said Abby. "Enjoy your lunch. After we grab a bite, Sam and I will be here through the noon hour to answer any questions you might have about this morning's session."

CHAPTER 13

Burn Baby Burn
Tuesday–7:37 PM

C harlie scanned the dimly lit dining room. They were back at Anthony's, and Gordon and Abby were already seated at a corner table. Easing his way through the crowded restaurant, he was drawn to Abby's smile. He'd love to be dining here alone with her, but the drama with Joe really did require Gordon's presence. *Besides,* thought Charlie, *What would you do if you did get her alone? Stutter all over your soup, that's what.* Of all the women he knew, only Abby still had that effect on him.

"Charlie, you look exhausted," said Gordon. "Have a seat."

"I am pretty beat. A full day of sessions can really take it out of a guy."

"Mm-hmm," agreed Gordon. "After we lost Joe, I thought there'd be this gaping hole in the group, like the elephant in the room no one talks about. But people really stepped up to the plate and participated."

"You do have a great group of people working with you, Gordon," said Charlie. "I think they'll be up for some extraordinary work back at the ranch. Tomorrow will be the real test, when we work on goals and commitments. It's easy to come up with all kinds of great goals when you're away from the office, but making them stick when you get home, that's the hard part, especially if you're in an organization that's hamstrung by policies and procedures. Sometimes upper management makes it difficult when staff returns from something like this and want to challenge the process."

"Luckily for ALMR, I'm not a big fan of outdated policies that hinder creativity and productivity," said Gordon.

"You've got to tell Charlie the barbecue story, Gordon," Abby said.

"Actually," chuckled Gordon, "the story starts with Abby. I was at one of her workshops several years ago, and she told a story about how her mentor had taught her to challenge the status quo by finding the useless activities in people's day and freeing them from that insanity . . . so I took that idea and went one better. I held an encouragement celebration by having a staff barbecue," Gordon laughed.

"Lots of people do that," said Charlie.

"Not with the policy and procedures manual as kindling, they don't," Gordon shot back. "I even went Sam and his time-keeping one better. I set up the whole scene in the parking lot. Staff wandered out as I held the manual over my head. I told them for too long we have argued about how we should do things, but we never asked why. 'Well, today,' I said, 'we start questioning everything. We will embrace change.' I doused the manual with lighter fluid. Then with great fanfare I tossed it into the black kettle grill and touched a match to it. The burst of flame danced in the stunned eyes of the silent crowd. And then one by one they started to cheer. Hotdogs and burgers never tasted so good."

"That's a terrific story, Gordon," Charlie laughed. "Abby never told me that one. Can I use it in my shtick? I'm headed to New York later this week. I'd love to use it in my next speech out there if that's OK with you."

"Be my guest," said Gordon.

"What's the deal in New York?" asked Abby, hoping her curiosity didn't come off as too interested.

"My agent got me this gig speaking to an insurance crowd. I haven't been to New York for a while and I'm really looking forward to it, especially to staying at the Waldorf."

"Does the coast-to-coast travel ever get to you?" Gordon asked.

"Sometimes," said Charlie, "especially when I'm going from airport to airport and staying in cheap hotels. However, I get to come to places like La Mariposa or the Waldorf and it's a real treat. I really love the job, and the travel just comes with the territory."

"You have to love it to put up with the kind of pressure that comes from situations like the one we had today," said Abby. "What are you going to do about Joe? Did he say anything to you after he left, Gordon?"

"Not much—he was pretty worked up. He did accuse us of trying to use the LPI to make him quit. Thought we'd set him up to humiliate him into resigning."

"That's not uncommon," Charlie said. "When the peer and supervisor evaluations come back and they're really off from the person's self-evaluation, there's a real tendency to look for any excuse rather than face the fact it might be true."

"It certainly wasn't our intention to force him out with the results of his leadership analysis, but I wouldn't be completely honest if I didn't say we haven't thought about letting him go," said Gordon. "Our HR director has been working with a recruiting agency to keep our feelers out there. They've been courting someone from a bigger firm, trying to arrange an interview, but so far nothing's come of it."

"Do you think he'll actually quit?" asked Abby. "From what I understand, he brought in most of your top accounts and is connected to just about every other project in some way."

"I know. We really don't want to lose him, but we can't exactly use him where he's at either."

"If you want my professional opinion, you need to give him some time." Charlie reached for the bread and passed the basket. He was starving. "Let him cool off tonight and then we can try to talk to him tomorrow. If you're serious about replacing him, though, you need to put your cards on the table. There's only so much we can do at an offsite like this—but I'm sure we can set you up with an executive coach if you want to rehab him. Make that a condition of staying. Otherwise, share the vision and politely ask him to get on board or consider another option that might be a better fit."

"Speaking of vision," added Gordon, "can we shift our focus for a bit? I want to pick your brain on a few things."

"Shoot," said Charlie.

"When I hear you talk about leadership, you're pretty much preaching to the choir," said Gordon, "but getting it to stick with the team, I think that's going to be a challenge. I'm running out of team-building ideas. We've done all the ordinary stuff. Have you got anything that qualifies as extraordinary?"

"What's the general attitude at ALMR right now?" Charlie asked.

"Well as a whole, we're pretty small potatoes to be competing in the market we're in," explained Gordon. "We've only got a few hundred employees. But that's still too big to have everyone be up close and personal with everyone else. And the industry's been in a bit of a slump, so there's been talk of mergers. When we first entertained the idea of partnering with ABP, a lot of our people were concerned. I think many of them still are. I'm hoping that these three days together show them it really is going to be a partnership and not an acquisition. Still, it's tough to get them to move beyond the superficial.

"This partnership deal is putting a lot of extra pressure on everyone and we have got to take a stand and define a new framework. But I'm afraid I'm running out of ideas. I've been researching some of the other vendors out there, but most of their stuff is routine. Perhaps an outdoor high ropes course. That might be fun and enlightening." It was more of a question than a statement.

"I think words like *fun* and *enlightening* might be part of the problem," replied Abby. "Real teams create communities and those fun things tend to follow naturally with time. It sounds like what's really going on is you're tired of people going to sessions like these and coming away with no real method for measuring results. You've spent all this money and traveled all this way only to see very little long-term impact for them as individuals or for the company—or for the community for that matter."

"So how can we change our focus?" asked Gordon. "I want to create a workplace that keeps the best of the team building, like the bonding that happens at an offsite like this. However, I want something that has a measurable impact on the organization in some bottom-line or brand-awareness sense. And if it does some good for the community that we live in—and do business in—so much the better."

"We've tried programs like what you're describing with some of our other clients," said Charlie. "Perhaps we could modify one of those for you. The one that resonates with me was called 'Building Responsibility, Building Teams, Building Community.' Kind of a cumbersome title, but the basic idea was to create a new partnership with the community by giving a hand instead of just a handout. The CEO used it as an integral part of their internal team building, but with a focus outward, to create an active, responsible citizenship in their local communities. Plus, it really connects to The Five Practices leadership model. Shows how the words can be turned into commitment. Deepens the learning. Keeps the effort alive, if you will."

"Sounds like an HR dream," said Gordon. "My brain's running a mile a minute on ideas already." He grabbed a pen and a notepad from his briefcase and started scribbling down ideas. "Would we be able to include our customer base in the process?" he asked.

"No reason why not," replied Charlie. "If you're serious about this, Gordon, I'll get you the contact information for the company I mentioned. Get you in touch with their CEO to ask more questions."

"That'd be great." Gordon's cell phone jangled from his jacket pocket. "Gordon Murphy." There was a long pause as he listened to someone on the line. "I've got to take this," he mouthed to Charlie and Abby, excusing himself from the table.

A thin veil of silence fell between them. Charlie shifted uncomfortably in his chair. For all the times he wanted to get her alone, he didn't know what to do now. *Say something, Stupid.* But Abby broke the silence first.

"You know, Charlie, there's something I've been meaning to tell you." She leaned forward, gazing straight into his eyes.

Here we go, thought Charlie. He felt sweat gathering on his brow. He wondered whether she could see it.

"What I wanted to say, was . . . is . . . "

"Yeah?"

Abby hesitated. *What am I doing?* She asked herself. *He's looking at you so expectantly, as though his life depended on your next few words, whatever they might be.* She didn't know herself. It had seemed like forever since she'd last seen Charlie, and she was bothered by the fact that she found she had missed him. A life constantly on the road was difficult. It was next to impossible to develop meaningful friendships with anyone, not to mention sustaining a real relationship. But that was the sacrifice she had made to get where she was in her business. Even though she realized she was drawn to Charlie on a personal level, there was nothing she could do about it. Her career meant too much to risk it all for a broken heart, either hers or . . . she didn't want to think it, but it wouldn't go away: Dennis's.

"Tomorrow at 5:15 sounds fine," Thankfully, Gordon interrupted the moment as he returned to their table. "Thank you very much." He flicked the phone shut and slid it back into his pocket. "Did I miss anything important?"

"Who was on the phone?" asked Abby with relief. Get a grip, she said to herself. Cover with a question. She could feel Charlie's gaze on her. She couldn't . . . wouldn't . . . make eye contact again.

"Believe it or not, it was the recruiter," said Gordon. "She's found someone she wants us to meet, and you're never going to believe this part." He paused for effect. "It's Gwen Kelly."

"Seriously?" Abby sputtered. "Gwen from ABP?"

"Well, that's certainly an interesting little twist," said Charlie, struggling to regain his composure.

"It is indeed," said Gordon. "I'm going to sit down with her tomorrow night for an informal interview."

"Isn't that going to rock the boat on the whole ABP–ALMR partnership?" asked Abby. "They're not going to be any too fond of you if you scoop up their director of sales."

"I'm just as surprised as you are, so I haven't had time to think it all through yet. In light of Joe's behavior today, I do think I should go forward with the informal interview, but I think we need to keep this under our hats for now." The two speakers nodded.

"Speaking of Joe," said Charlie. "Has anybody seen him since he left the session today?"

"He was headed outside when he left me," Gordon replied. "I haven't seen him since. He's probably somewhere blowing off a little steam. I'm not worried, but I think I'll leave a message for him at the front desk, just in case he tries to check out early. If you'll excuse me, I think I'm going to head back to my room." Turning to Charlie and adopting a fatherly tone he said, "I trust the two of you will get home at a decent hour?"

If he only knew, thought Charlie. He turned to Abby. "So what did you want to tell me?"

Abby took a desperate sip of water. Her throat was so dry.

"N-nothing," she stammered. "Nothing except I think you're doing a terrific job."

CHAPTER 14

To Dream, Perhaps
Tuesday—10:14 PM

Charlie had been surprised when Abby agreed to have a nightcap with him.

He ordered two Irish coffees and met Abby by the pool. *God, she's beautiful sitting there in the starlight,* he thought. But what had that been all about at dinner? Why make such a big deal about telling him he was doing a good job? Was it possible that Abby felt the same way about him that he felt about her? Was that what she had wanted to say? In all the years he had known Abby, Charlie had never seen her at such a loss for words. Abby was the consummate professional, the consummate career woman. He'd always respected that about her. *So what now?* he wondered. And yet, here they were at the poolside on a beautiful desert night, a slight breeze in the air, the moon reflected in ripples in the water.

"I'm flying out of here tomorrow night to New York," he said, handing Abby her coffee and sitting across from her on a deck chair. "Who knows when our paths will cross again?"

Abby still couldn't bring herself to meet his gaze.

"There'll be other conferences, Charlie," she said, sipping her drink. *Why am I sitting here?* she asked herself. She was exhausted and all she really wanted was a hot bath and her bed. She'd give Dennis another call too: tell him she was still considering his proposal but needed more time. It didn't feel right to her to be entertaining notions of pursuing a relationship with Charlie with Dennis's proposal hanging over her conscience. "Vegas, Chicago, Orlando, D.C. I'm sure we're bound to run into each other at one of those."

"Ah yes," Charlie sighed wistfully. "Our lives as motivational speakers: always living out of a suitcase. Always on the road...."

"It's the choice we made," Abby suddenly snapped.

"But don't you ever get tired of it?" Charlie asked. "Don't you ever get, I don't know, lonely?"

Lonely. Abby sighed, shook her head, and took another sip of coffee. The whisky had a calming effect, she noted, but it also made her feel vulnerable. It was Charlie's fault, she decided. Vulnerability was not something she allowed herself to feel very often.

"Pushing the personal button again, Charlie," she said. *If only he knew,* she thought. *Or perhaps he does?* Abby refused to even consider it.

"We're friends, aren't we?" Charlie countered. "What were you going to tell me at dinner, before Gordon interrupted you?"

"Nothing," she said. "I told you. You're doing a great job. That's it."

"I don't believe you," he said pushing the button a bit harder.

He loved the way her neck curved into a delicate hollow. He wanted to run his fingers through her hair, down her back, around her waist. *God, this is so wrong,* he thought. But the fact he sensed—he knew—Abby was attracted to him too seemed to make everything OK.

"I don't care whether you believe it or not," Abby said, surprised by the level of hostility entering her voice. "You know as well as I do that nothing can ever happen between us." *Jackpot!* Charlie thought.

But Abby wasn't a game. "Listen, Charlie, there's something I probably should tell you."

Charlie grinned. "That you find me irresistible as hell?" he said.

Abby sighed. "No," she replied. "I'm engaged. . . . I mean, I'm about to be engaged. I mean. . . ." She waited for Charlie's reaction but he just sat there, looking at her like he'd been hit by a semi. It thoroughly unnerved her. *Spin,* she thought, *just spin.* "And besides, we're professionals, Charlie. I haven't worked this hard to get where I am to let it all go to hell over some foolish tryst with a coworker. My professional integrity is the most important thing I have, Charlie. I'm not going to let romantic feelings or attraction or whatever you want to call it get in the way of what I've accomplished. Not now, especially not now."

"So what's his name?" Charlie asked. The question sounded almost like an accusation.

"What?"

"His name? The sad sap who proposed to you?"

"Dennis," she said. Just saying his name to Charlie felt like a betrayal. "Look, we're always telling people they need to make appropriate choices in their lives and they need to stick to their values. What good are we—the choice agents—when we can't even stick to our own choices? Well, I believe in what I do. And if I can't practice what I preach, then what good am I? What good are any of us?"

"Come to New York with me."

This she hadn't expected. "What? Charlie, no, haven't you been listening to me?"

"Come to New York. Obviously this Dennis guy . . . we wouldn't be having this conversation if you were sure you wanted to be with him for the rest of your life. Come to New York and see how you feel about him after a couple days with me."

"No!" Abby got up from her chair and hurried back into the hotel before Charlie had even a chance of catching her. She heard him calling out to her but she didn't stop. In the elevator, she burst into tears. Charlie was right. If she really loved Dennis. . . .

Alone in her room, Abby slipped the velvet box out of her briefcase and took another look at the ring. It certainly was beautiful. Dennis had surprised her with it at dinner the night before she left for Tucson, sliding the box across the table during dessert. Abby slipped the ring onto her finger and admired its glitter in the light from the bedside lamp. It spun its colors across the hotel room ceiling as if Tinker Bell herself had flown into the room. Dennis was certainly a charmer, but was he Prince Charming? He was so unsure of himself.

Enough. Abby hurled the box across the bed and flopped down beside it. *Congratulations, Abby!* she cried to herself. *You've done it. You've let your guard down for the first time in God knows how many years. How does it feel? Horrible.* She realized that no amount of career success could ever again mask the fact that she was bored. *And try as hard as you can to keep it all together, to claim it doesn't matter, it does. Dennis is the safe choice. He can give you the security you need: a stable, loving home, a haven to return to from endless days and weeks on the road. But what he can't give you is passion. And that's what's lacking most from your life. Passion. And Charlie is, well, all about passion. So, what's it going to be?*

Abby buried her face in the pillow and sobbed herself to sleep.

The noise from an adjoining room woke Charlie. He squinted at the hotel-issue alarm clock and its ruby-red news, 3:21 AM. He needed to pee. Fighting the desire, he burrowed under his pillow, but nature won. Dragging his legs off the edge of the bed, he felt a bit dizzy. He hadn't had that much to drink at dinner. Still, he couldn't put it back the way he could when he was younger. He stumbled to the bathroom door with his eyes half closed. He knew these hotel rooms like the back of his hand. The heavy door slammed behind him, jarring him from his stupor. Charlie gasped. He wasn't in his hotel room bathroom, he was in the brightly lit hallway. Spinning around, Charlie pushed at the door to his room. Locked! But being locked out wasn't the biggest problem. No, the biggest problem was that Charlie slept in the buff. Naked as a jaybird.

Charlie's eyes darted down the hallway. There were no plants or chairs or anything that could hide him. The only idea that sprang to mind was to run like hell to the elevators and use the house phone to call the front desk. "Please God, let a male clerk answer," he gasped, making a mad dash down the hallway. Just as he was about to round the bend in the hallway, the elevator rang its arrival and voices came hustling down the hall toward him. Doing a 180-degree turn in midair, Charlie raced back down the hall and hid behind an emergency exit door. Hopping up and down on the chilly concrete floor reminded him of what started this escapade. He really had to pee. "Hurry up," he hissed as the couple fumbled for their keys. Stupid people in love. They were stopping to kiss when they should be getting out of the damn hall!

When the coast was clear, Charlie, cupping himself firmly, repeated his run for the elevators. Reaching for the phone on the lobby table, he prayed the elevator wouldn't arrive again, because this time he was totally without cover.

"You've reached the reception desk. How may I direct your call?"

What should he say now? "I've locked myself out of my room and I'm wondering if you could send someone up to let me in."

"Jeni will be right there, sir. What room are you in?"

"Uhhhhh, it's room number 362, but I'd rather you send a man. I'm in a bit of a predicament. I wasn't exactly dressed when I ended up in the hallway instead of the bathroom and . . ."

"I understand sir. I'll send a gentleman up immediately."

"Thank you!"

Charlie ran back down the hallway and repositioned himself behind the emergency exit door. The clerk arrived, slid the card into its slot and propped the door open. When he turned his back to the door, Charlie scooted in behind him. "Thank you," he shouted, safe from the other side.

"Don't mention it, sir," said the young man with a smirk. "I know I wouldn't."

Charlie awoke with a start. The dream. He took a deep breath to steady his pounding heart and squinted at the clock: 3:21 AM. He'd only been asleep for a few hours. The dream rarely snuck up on him that fast. He'd always written it off as a travel nightmare. Spend enough time in hotels and sooner or later . . . well, he hoped the dream would stay just that, a dream. It always made him feel vulnerable. Not that he didn't feel that way already. The evening with Abby had left him feeling exposed. Exposed and angry. He hadn't misread the signs. *She's into you,* he thought, punching at his pillows to create a mound behind his head. How long had it been since that had happened?

Four years, three months, and some odd days. And he was still angry with Sarah for the way it had ended. Charlie hadn't had a lot of intimate relationships, but Sarah had been the one, his soul mate, at least it had seemed that way at first. She was the kind of woman for whom you'd buy tickets to a traveling exhibit of Renoir paintings, or at least buy new sheets, and he'd done both. *Beautiful, intelligent, confident, a lot like Abby,* thought Charlie. But Sarah's list had expanded to clingy and controlling.

She didn't like his travel schedule, how he "always gave his time to others and never to her." Moving in together had been her idea, "so that we can see each other whenever you are home," she explained. *I should've drawn the line right there, because next she was fishing for a ring, and a wedding, and kids, and oh my gawd, she was suffocating.*

"I'll never fall into that trap again," swore Charlie under his breath. And he'd never let anyone get close. His cowboy lifestyle was just what the doctor ordered. Never in one place for long, spending his nights alone in a sparse hotel room sequestered only with his thoughts. But now his thoughts kept swirling around Abby Bancroft. All these years they'd known each other, boiled down to one embarrassing and, yes, painful scene by a pool under a desert sky. Could it get that much more clichéd? Of one thing Charlie was certain, he wasn't about to make the same mistake again.

CHAPTER 15

Our Never-Ending Story

Wednesday–8:53 AM

Gwen had hoped to catch a few minutes with Jerry before the start of the session, but it had been a crazy morning. She'd been up half the night thinking about her meeting with Gordon and had forgotten to request a wake-up call. She'd barely had time to shower and dress before grabbing a bagel and landing in her seat. *Gordon must know by now that I'm the candidate,* she thought. *I wonder what he thinks of all this?*

Abby also spun into the room as if caught in a personal tornado. She hardly slept a wink the night before, thinking about Charlie and what she'd said to him. Had she been too tough on him? She'd been accused in the past of being an ice goddess, although she'd honestly never seen herself that way: just focused, determined. Her determination had helped her reach the top of her game even though perhaps it had prevented her from connecting with anyone on a more personal level. Why were men who were tough in business considered successful, and women who were equally tough considered bitches? Abby had never understood the double standard. And damn it, she did like Charlie. She liked him a lot. Maybe it was his energy. Or perhaps it was how she melted when he casually touched her. Whatever it was, she knew that Charlie was the best she'd ever worked with, after Sam of course. And now she'd run the risk of alienating him. What would she do then? *But I can't think about that right now,* she told herself, scanning the room for Sam. *We have another session ahead of us. I need to focus. Focus, Abby.*

She found Sam by the coffee and donuts. "Sam, we're running late. We need to get started."

Sam just looked at her like she'd risen from the dead. He chugged the coffee down.

"You OK, Abby?" he asked.

"Yeah, sorry, " Abby stammered. "I'm fine, thanks. I'm just eager to get started, that's all."

"Let's get it going, then," Sam replied.

"Good morning!" Sam beamed as people settled into their seats. "I hope you had a chance to enjoy our beautiful surroundings last night. I just love Arizona this time of year." Murmurs of approval wove through the room. "Now that you've had some time to think about The Five Practices of Exemplary Leadership, I want to move you forward into what we call *The Never-Ending Story Community Building Extravaganza.* It sounds like a mouthful, but that just might mean that it's easier to do than it is to say," said Sam with a grin. *God, it feels good to be back in the saddle.* The teaching at U of A was fulfilling, but those kids were so young. They had no idea what awaited them, and he sometimes had a hard time selling them on the importance of leadership. But these people, this team was battle-weary and thirsting for it. He could see it on their faces.

"The worst thing that you can do when you leave here tomorrow is nothing," said Abby. "Through this next session, we want to give you enough detail and enough examples so you can take the efforts you'll start here today and carry them forward. In fact, when you get back to the ranch, we suggest you set up a mini-offsite for the rest of your staff."

"Take your groups and split them into two camps," explained Sam. "With the first group, give them the challenge of identifying everything that is currently going on with their particular part of the organization, or with the organization as a whole, depending on your perspective. Their responsibility is to accurately, honestly, and specifically capture the reality of today's story, even if it isn't very flattering."

"That's a key point," added Abby. "It's very important that this team lay out the good and the bad and even the ugly. If they paint a false picture of the present situation, then any efforts to change it will be based on an illusion, and that's just pointless— like giving a cancer patient a Band-Aid. Keep in mind, though, that this autopsy, if you will, isn't an attack."

"While the first group is engrossed in the present story, the second group will be engaged in 'brainstorying' the future story," explained Sam. "You've probably never heard of brainstorying before—I made it up. It's a cross between brainstorming and storytelling. You see, brainstorming gets the ideas flowing and people start thinking, but I don't think that's enough. Too many times people walk away from a brainstorming session with no real vision. But storytelling, that's where the vision piece falls into place. You see, storytelling isn't just an exercise in hope. Storytelling is action-oriented. I don't remember who said it, but as someone once told me, 'Action without vision is labor; vision without action is lottery; but action with vision creates your legacy.'"

"While the present story team looks at reality, the future story team should focus on what you want to move toward," added Abby. "A future story should take anywhere from six months to a year to achieve, and it should also be specific. Don't just say, 'We want to do better,' or 'We want to sell more.' Ask specific questions: How do we want to be, look, and act? What do we want to start doing? Stop doing? Do more of? Do less of? What are our priorities? And how should we celebrate success?"

"You want to create an attitude of gratitude," said Sam.

"If you are the titled leader," Abby continued, "be sure that you seed the conversation but do not direct the content. If you do, the team will only parrot back what you want and the process will be thwarted."

"You'll eventually need to pull the two groups back together to actually tell their stories. Give everyone a chance to chime in and share their two cents so they all become owners of the current reality and the future story."

"This is where the titled leader gets to step back in," said Abby. "You're going to take action, by picking up a metaphorical sledgehammer and smashing the future story into chunks. These chunks are the steps necessary to achieve the future story. Then ask the team to place them into a priority from first step to last step. Don't worry if they don't fall into a straight line. It's sort of like putting a jigsaw puzzle together. You might have steps that are linear, or overlapping, or even parallel. What's critical is that the team understands all the pieces and how they fit into the big future story."

"And once you have the chunks, it is time to find the champions. The Chunk Champs!" said, Sam raising his arms in a classic Rocky pose. That got a laugh. "Each chunk or puzzle piece needs to have someone in the group, but *not* the titled leader, become its champion. Then others in the group can sign on as chunk supporters, or Chunkies, including the titled leader. The Chunk Champ and Chunkies then break the chunk into pebbles: the individual smaller tasks that need to be accomplished so you can achieve the chunk. And here's where it really picks up steam, because when each chunk is accomplished, you celebrate and each celebration brings you closer to the big dance, when the future story becomes the present reality and your goal is achieved."

"Ah, but if you think that's the end, then you've forgotten this is the never-ending story!" Abby laughed. "Once you reach your goal and your team has had a chance to revel in their success, you bring them back together and pull out the old flip charts and draw a line from the old Future Story box to a new box titled Next Future Story. So the old future story becomes the current reality, and the process starts all over again. It's not a program or an agenda imposed on you by someone else. It's your people carrying out their own ideas toward their own goals."

"And," added Sam, "the Extravaganza was created to match perfectly with the LPI we covered yesterday afternoon. The

Never-Ending Story process supports each and every behavior posed in the report. So, if you really want to improve your leadership behavior and increase your scores, I suggest you embrace the Never-Ending Story process."

"We've been doing an awful lot of the talking this morning," said Sam, as he and Abby finished sharing some real-life stories from folks who'd embraced the process. "I'd like to hear from you guys." People shuffled in their seats. A woman in the back raised her hand. "Go ahead," Sam encouraged.

"I really like the ideas that you guys are giving us," she said. "I mean, the whole process sounds really great, but it seems like all of the companies in these stories had an idea of where they wanted to go."

"Yeah," said a man near the front. "It's like they already had a vision or a direction and we really don't."

Sam nodded. "I think you might be forgetting about the brainstorying part. The people in our stories created their own visions. Some were big, others small. A vision doesn't have to be something heroic or huge, but it does have to be shared. However you approach it, just remember to stop saying yes to mediocre and start saying yes to magnificent. And if you think Abby and I are going to let you get away from these sessions without a little brainstorying of your own, well, then you didn't read the fine print." Sam smiled. They really were a great group. With the right leadership and the right future story, they'd be an amazing sales force.

"We're about out of time for this morning," said Abby. "Jerry's going to come up and give you some direction on this afternoon's sessions. Jerry. . . ."

"Thanks Abby, and Sam," Jerry said, moving to the front of the room. "I think you've definitely got our wheels turning this morning. After lunch, we're going to put some traction on this, so here's the plan."

The room erupted into a flurry of activity as Jerry outlined the process and the timing for their small group brainstorying. People really started to open up as they headed for the dining area.

Gwen joined Sam and Abby at the front of the room, careful to avoid Jerry. "So how do you think it's going so far?" she asked.

"It looks like they're still soaking it all in," said Sam. "I'll be very interested to see what they come back with this afternoon."

"I'll second that," said Abby. "This is a lot of information to digest in one sitting. When they actually start working through the action steps, I think it'll make more sense."

"You know, you're really the titled leader for this team, Gwen," Sam added. "In this exercise I'd like to see you take a bigger role this afternoon."

"I don't know." Gwen hesitated. "There's been a lot of tension between me and the team. I think it might actually hinder the process if I take the lead."

"But you are their leader, Gwen," said Abby. "If you don't want to tackle those issues here, it's not going to get any easier at home. At some point, you've got to decide if you're going to make the move from manager to leader."

"I'm trying, I really am," Gwen said defensively. "It's not as easy as you guys make it out to be."

"I don't think anyone ever promised that it would be easy," said Sam gently. "Only that it will become more natural. I think that's the experience that the three of us share." Abby nodded in agreement.

"OK," Gwen sighed. "If you think that's best, I'll lead the exercise. I just don't think I have a lot of credibility right now."

"Then this is the perfect thing," said Sam. "What better way to build that credibility than by stepping up as a leader through the Never-Ending Story process."

"In that case, I'm going to take a quiet lunch to prepare," said Gwen, gathering her notes and purse. "I'll see you two at two-thirty."

CHAPTER 16

A Rope; A Hope
Wednesday–7:14 AM

Joe heard a low moan, his own, echo through the thick darkness. The intensity of his own sound startled him. Pain swept through him. *Where am I?* He felt the chilly stone under his cheek and shuddered at the memory of the fall. How long had it been? His shallow ragged breaths came in spurts. *Slow down, buddy.* There was no sound, no light, no hope.

"Hello?" he cried into the darkness. Nothing but his echo returned. The group must be long gone by now. They'd left him. Just like his father, just like Nora. The darkness shrouded his body like a tomb. He was completely and utterly alone.

Joe shifted his weight and gripped the cave floor as the pain clouded his mind. Could he move his arms? His legs? Should he? Paralyzed by fear, he closed his eyes and drifted back into the darkness of his mind.

He woke again, maybe hours later, less confused but just as scared. Gritting his teeth, Joe moved his left arm and then his right. Both answered him. His legs didn't appear to be broken either. In fact, nothing seemed to be broken except his spirit. Pulling himself into a sitting position, Joe reached out to the floor around him, it was solid, but who knew where the next drop could be. . . .

"Oh god," he moaned into the hollow air. "Why me? What have I ever done to you?" His complaints echoed through the cave, fueling his anger. It was Gordon's fault for making him come. Charlie's fault for driving him away from the group. Nora's fault for leaving. Anything to take away the pain of being alone. His mind was spinning now. How long had it been since the tour left? Was anyone looking for him? *Surely, they'll notice I'm not there for dinner.* If there'd even been a dinner yet. Or what if there'd already been several. The chilling truth crept over him as he realized he could be trapped down here for days, maybe already had been. His stomach roared with hunger and his lungs cried out for a cigarette. *I'd kill for a smoke right about now,* he thought, reaching for his breast pocket. Just a smashed up cigarette box.

His hands felt their way around until one bumped the steel of one of the many ladders that had taken him down into the caves. He managed to climb the twelve rungs to the next level. He got to the top and slumped to his knees again. His hands rested on the ground for a few seconds, then his left hand slid forward. The lighter! He'd found the lighter he'd dropped right before he fell, just lying there on the floor. Joe snatched the lighter and desperately flicked at it. *Slow down now. Take it easy.* He ran his thumb over the small canister and gave the spark wheel another flick. Light erupted, casting eerie shadows on the walls. He glanced at his watch. No good. The face had been smashed by the fall. But at least he could see a little way around him.

Guided by the tiny light Joe rose gingerly and limped toward the cave wall. Leaning back against it, he snapped the lighter closed and gasped once again in the darkness. How much fuel was left in the lighter? And what about the flint? How long would it last? He'd have to conserve the light even if it meant facing the darkness. He had to get out of the dark. But which way to go? Abby's words flickered through his memory. Something about a cat from *Alice in Wonderland,* about ending up somewhere or going nowhere.

"I want to get out of here," he yelled. Feeling along the wall, he sensed a path to his left. Taking his first real steps since the fall, Joe shuffled forward. *Not very Indiana Jones,* he thought, pausing every few steps to catch his breath. How did those movie guys make this cave stuff look so easy? Always dodging traps and leaping onto bridges that only appeared by faith.

Faith, thought Joe. *That's what I need.* His mother had filled his childhood with stories of faith. Why couldn't he remember any of them now? It didn't matter, he was living by faith. Faith there would be a next step and not a plunging hole. "Trust the process," he heard Gordon say in the back of his mind. He snorted. *I don't think this is exactly what Gordon had in mind,* he thought.

Flicking the lighter every few feet, Joe inched along the wall for what seemed like hours. Rounding another bend in the path, Joe stared at the open space in front of him. "Shit." He'd been going in circles. There was the pile of rubble from his fall just below. "Get me out of here," he hollered into the darkness. Swiping at tears of frustration, Joe realized that he was no longer afraid of the dark. He was afraid of death. No one had heard him. He was exhausted. His body still throbbed from the impact. He had no idea how to save himself.

A chill of rejection crept into his soul. There really was no one coming to get him. He leaned against the wall and sobbed. Slumping to the floor, he longed for comfort, for Nora's arms. For even a shadow of the past to wrap its arms around him and tell him everything would be OK, that this was just a bad dream, that soon he would wake up in his own bed. Fatigue nipped around the corners of his mind, but he dared not give in. If he closed his eyes, even for a moment, he might not be able to open them again. *Let it go, Joe,* he thought. *Just close your eyes and it will all be over. No more marriage problems, no more heartache, no more work, no more pretending to be something you're not. Just close your eyes and say good-bye to all of it.*

"No!" He screamed into the darkness, gasping for air as the thoughts crushed at his chest. "Just give me another chance. I'm just a fake. I can see that now. Please give me another chance and I'll make it right." He thought about Nora and all the pain he'd caused her. The way he'd blamed it all on her; the infertility, his infidelity, his inability to love her. "It was all my fault," he sobbed. "And Gordon and Charlie. They didn't do this to me. I did it to myself. I chose this life. I chose this attitude. I chose to ignore what everyone else could see." Joe reached out his hands in the darkness, tears streaming down his face. "Forgive me!" he shouted into the darkness. "I forgive you. Please forgive me!" His heart pounded in his chest. He was growing dizzy. Years of fear and frustration drained from his body. He threw his head back and laughed. What was that strange euphoria washing over his soul? He'd forgotten that feeling, the lightness, the peace. It was joy. And something else. A shimmer of light.

Joe stared at the light. It didn't move. "It must be real," he gasped. Ignoring his pain, he hurled himself toward it. Within a few minutes, Joe saw the mouth of the cave path. He was growing weaker with each step. "Hang in there, buddy," he whispered. His leg brushed against a guide rope and his heart surged with hope. If he could follow the rope, surely it would lead to freedom. But the strain was too much for his weary limbs. He collapsed in a heap at the side of the path.

Raul, one of the guides from Colossal Caves, set out on his early morning preparation for the day of tourists ahead. He moved to the entrance of the cave and gathered up the lanterns to replace the batteries and get them ready for the new day. He looked down and noticed a cigarette butt just outside the cave. "That's strange," he said aloud. Cigarette smoking was not allowed, and the guides always made a point of asking their groups not to smoke well before they got to this point.

He took his flashlight and walked into the cave to see if he noticed anything else unusual. A shadow caught the corner of his eye and Raul realized that he wasn't alone. "Who's there?" he called into the stillness.

Joe opened his eyes to a blaze of light. Someone had turned the lights back on. "Help me," he rasped.

Raul ran toward the voice. It was a man covered in dirt. What had happened? "Sir, sir, are you all right? How did you get in here?"

"I fell." It was all the strength Joe had left.

Raul grabbed his radio. "Base camp, we've got an injured guy in the cave. Send down blankets and water and call 911." He knelt down beside Joe and reached for his hand. "You're going to be OK, sir."

When Joe came to, he was strapped to a stretcher in the back of an ambulance.

"Do you remember anything at all, sir?" asked the EMT.

"I was with a tour but I wasn't supposed to be on the tour and I fell into the cave," said Joe reaching for the water bottle the EMT held out. "How long was I down there?"

"The last tour left the cave around seven last night and it's almost nine now, so I'd say fourteen hours, at least."

Joe let his head fall back against the pillow. "Didn't think I was going to make it for a while there," he said.

"Other than some nasty bruises and dehydration, it looks like you're walking away from this one a lucky man."

"I am," said Joe. "I am. And I'm starting to feel almost human; any chance I could sit up a bit?"

The attendant cranked up the head of the stretcher and adjusted the straps so Joe could move his arms. "How's that?"

"Better. Not so trapped."

"We found a hotel key in your pocket, La Mariposa," the attendant said. "Is that where you're staying?"

"Yeah."

"Well that's good news," said the EMT. "There was a missing person report made last night by a group from there. It looks like you're the one they're looking for. Why don't you lean back and relax. We'll be at the hospital in about an hour and a half."

Joe gazed out the back window as the road unwound behind them. "If I never go cave hopping again, I think it will still be too soon," he murmured.

The EMT pulled a backpack out from under his seat. "Do you mind if I read on the road?" he asked Joe.

"Be my guest. What've you got in there?"

"Textbooks mostly. I'm a student at the U of A."

"Do you mind?" asked Joe, reaching for a nondescript white binder.

"Be my guest."

Joe settled back against the thin pillow of his stretcher and opened the binder. It was dog-eared and full of Post-it notes. He grazed over a few pages until his eyes rested on a line that compelled him to read with intensity:

Each of us hungers to create great work. It is something we are born with. It gnaws at us. Some try to ignore it through the mediocre and mundane. But thoughts of our legacy slip away in the quicksand of time.

My work certainly hasn't been great, thought Joe as the past few months played through his mind. *If Gordon is worth his salt*

as a CEO, he should fire me after what I've put them all through.
But was it really too late? Maybe. But he still owed Gordon an
apology. Turning the page, Joe read on:

> Many are asleep. They see life as a battleship, not a sailing
> ship. They see life as endurance, not engagement. They are
> blind to their destiny, with its ripple effects. They float shore
> to shore, only dreaming. Disturb their slumber.

This is exactly what Abby and Charlie are about, he thought,
soaking up the words. Charlie. There was another apology and
that one was going to be tough. The guy still rubbed him raw,
but he had been right all along. It was all about his attitude.
And the group, he'd really embarrassed himself there too. Not
just for yesterday, but for all the yesterdays before that.

> When you draw your future with your passion, stay focused
> so, you are not drawn off.

What am I passionate about? wondered Joe. He hadn't felt
anything but frustration and anger in a long, long time. *I don't
even know if I can get over all the garbage I've thrown in my own
path. Maybe Charlie could help me.* Joe read for the entire ride
back to the hospital. As they eased into the driveway he came
across a handwritten note on the inside back cover:

> Yesterday is your memory,
> Tomorrow your dream.

Today is your masterpiece,
Create it!

The EMT swung open the back doors. "Here we are." The sudden light startled Joe.

"Oh, right. This is quite a read," he said holding up the white binder. "Where'd you get it? I don't see a title or anything."

"It's actually a reader for one of my business courses. I think my prof wrote most of it."

"What's his name?" asked Joe.

"Sam Arthur. He's a real character."

CHAPTER 17

Fire Away!
Wednesday—11:11 AM

J oe had been in his hospital bed for about half an hour
when Gordon arrived.

He could see the nurse at the central station motion to
show Gordon where to find him. His pulse quickened as
his guilt descended on him.

"Took a bit of a tumble, but he's going to be OK," said the
nurse at Joe's bedside.

"Where? When?"

"I've been doing a little soul-searching at the bottom of
a cave," said Joe. "I was so mad when I left the session yesterday that I jumped on the first bus I saw to get the hell out
of here. Ended up on the Colossal Cave tour and knocked
myself out."

"You really had me worried, Joe."

"I'm sorry, Gordon. I wasn't thinking clearly. But I am now. I think we need to talk. I'm getting myself out of here. I'm fine and I want to set things straight as soon as possible."

"Absolutely, but you need to have them check you out first," Gordon replied.

"They have, and I'm fine, right?" he said looking up at the nurse. The nurse remained expressionless as a sign of approval. "See?" Joe said.

"I'll check myself out and we can go back and talk. Do you think Charlie could join us?" asked Joe.

"I'll certainly ask," said Gordon.

Back at the hotel later that day, Joe wrapped his hands around a coffee mug and inhaled the rich earthy scent. Everything seemed more vivid since he'd been pulled out of the cave. Gordon and Charlie exchanged bemused glances. "So what's on your mind, Joe?" asked Gordon as he dove into his Caesar salad.

"For starters, I need to apologize to you." Joe took a deep breath. "Since the day you started at ALMR I've been waiting for you to fail. No, more than that, I've been working toward your failure. I'm sure you know I interviewed for the CEO position. . . ."

"Yes, the board explained the situation when I interviewed," said Gordon.

"Well, when the board didn't pick me, it was a big blow to my ego. I pretty much made up my mind to hate you, and when you came in with your completely new leadership vision, well, that just ate me up. I've always thought of myself as a leader—but you were the real deal, and I was afraid that sooner or later, you'd reveal me for the poser I really was. But I think that honor really fell to you, Charlie."

"How so?" asked Charlie.

"Everything you said in your session yesterday, and a little bit from Abby earlier, it all hit home. I'm sorry for blowing up at you. You really are a catalyst and I realize now that when I was pissed off at you, I should have been angry with myself." Joe reached out his hand. "Please forgive me."

"Apology accepted," said Charlie, shaking his hand.

"I don't remember the last time I said this," said Joe hesitantly, "but I'm going to need some help."

"What do you need?" asked Gordon.

"I need help focusing on what really matters," said Joe. "I need to know how to actually do the stuff you guys talk about. I mean, assuming I still have a job." He looked at Gordon.

"If we're being honest here, Joe, I'm not one hundred percent sure. We've been watching you for a few months now, and you know as well as I do we've got enough to work with if it came down to letting you go."

"I know."

"Still, if you're serious about cleaning up your act, and you're willing to work one-on-one with an executive coach to deal with some of these attitude and behavioral problems, I think a probation period would be a reasonable solution," said Gordon. "Charlie, can PLC put together a program for us?"

"Abby can put together a process, Gordon," said Charlie. "Are you really ready to make some changes?" he asked Joe.

"I couldn't be more ready. I had quite a bit of time to think yesterday. Impending death really boils down the important stuff. I need to show up and speak up and all of those things. Otherwise, I might as well shut up and show myself to the door."

"That's a nifty little twist," chuckled Charlie. "I guess you really were paying attention."

"Oh, I don't have any problem with the hearing," said Joe. "It's the doing I've had a tough time with. I don't know what the hell I'm doing. I feel like I'm just shadowboxing with the truth."

"That doesn't make any sense," said Charlie. "All my information on you says that you're a great salesman. Why do you feel like a fake?"

"I am a great salesman, Charlie. I've been doing it all my life, it seems. Even when I was just a kid, I sold stuff in my dad's shop back in Ronkonkoma."

"You're from Ronkonkoma, New York?" Charlie sounded surprised.

"Yeah. Are you familiar with it?"

"I actually connected through there last year heading into New York," Charlie offered. "It's just strange I'd actually meet someone from there."

"It's a quiet little place. My dad had a small business there, and my brother and I used to work for him off and on," explained Joe. "So, I've been selling stuff forever, but I'm not good with managing a group." He paused. "The truth is, I have no real interest in managing a group."

"Then how did you get to be vice president of sales?" asked Gordon. "And why did you apply for my job?"

"I've been with ALMR forever and I just kept taking promotions when they became available. I mean, that's what you're supposed to do. Nobody respects someone who's held the same position for years and never moved up. Besides, with all these young guys entering the market, I didn't want to end up answering to someone younger and more successful than myself. So I kept moving up—and by the time I got out of the actual sales jobs, I was miserable. But it seemed stupid to ask for a demotion back into sales. I guess I got stuck. Then with the whole CEO thing, I figured if I was going to be miserable, at least I could be miserable at the top."

"You know we actually covered that idea in the session this morning," said Charlie. "I call it the 'Shoemaker Story' or the 'Cobbler Story.' It's my personal rant about how our society pushes people into positions of greater and greater responsibility even though they have no interest in moving up."

"Well, I can certainly identify with that," Joe replied. "What did you tell them?"

"The cobbler is really an artist. He has a passion for making shoes; working with his hands; working with leather. He doesn't want to be the CEO of a shoe conglomerate. He just wants to design and create shoes. But our society looks down at him. 'Why don't you want to be the head cobbler?' people ask, as if designing and creating isn't enough, as if he's a failure if he's not telling somebody else what to do. We put too much importance on the responsibility of managing larger and larger groups of people. Sure, it's the right path for some people, but not if it's at the cost of sacrificing what you love. In some ways, academia has it right. Professors don't usually want to be president of the university. They want to do their research or teach what they love to others."

"The corporate environment can really learn from that," Gordon added.

It was like Charlie could see right through him. "That's exactly it," said Joe as relief flooded his soul. "I've always felt pressured to move up, instead of being a better salesman. The further away I got from what I actually enjoyed doing, the more stressed-out my life became. Even though I was moving up, it felt like I was being beaten down."

"Exactly," Charlie said. "As leaders, we need to stop that kind of insanity. I think that when people learn how to remove the power trip from the management side of things, everyone could relax a bit. Many people end up doing work they hate while living in fear of upsetting the boss," Charlie continued. "I always wonder how grown adults can let other adults yell at them and treat them poorly and rationalize it all due to the mortgage payment."

"That sounds a lot like your suck versus success line," Joe added.

"Boy, you really were paying attention the other day," said Gordon.

"More than you might think."

Charlie surveyed the changed man before him. It really was remarkable. Not everyone needs to fall into a pit to begin making different choices in life, but moments like this made everything, the busy airports, clunky rental cars, and cheap hotels, worth it. "It sounds like you're ready, Joe. I know you're going to get into some serious coaching in the future, but can I give you a few pointers to get you started?"

"I'm game for anything. Fire away."

CHAPTER 18

The Brainstory
Wednesday—2:12 PM

G wen glanced at her watch. Fifteen minutes until the beginning of the next session. *How am I ever going to pull this off?* Telling Jerry about the interview with Gordon had been much more difficult than she'd anticipated. He'd been professional, as always, but she could see the disappointment in his face. *God, I'm tired of disappointing people.*

"Gwen?" Sam laid a hand on her arm. She hadn't heard him enter the meeting room.

"Yes?"

"I know you can do this." Sam smiled. "You're so close to becoming a leader, but something's holding you back. I don't know what it is, and I don't really need to. But you're going to have to figure it out."

"I know," Gwen sighed. "There's just so much to think about right now."

"Well I'll make you a deal," Sam offered. "For the next few hours, you only have to think about the people in this room. You've been their director for two years. Today, I want you to be their leader. If you can help them see the vision, they'll join up with you."

"Thank you, Sam."

"Anytime. It looks like everyone's back from their brainstorying sessions. Why don't you go ahead and get started. Abby and Jerry and I are all here for you."

Gwen cleared her throat and faced the room. "Welcome back, everyone. I hope you had some productive brainstorming time this afternoon. We're going to spend the next few hours looking at our current situation and trying to put together our future story. It's not a big secret that our sales are down and this is affecting our morale and team motivation. I believe that Sam and Abby have given us the tools to do something about that. So this afternoon we're going to take ownership of the situation and create a new, more positive, future story. I'd like to start with the present story team. Why don't you folks take the floor and outline where you believe we are today?"

Brad Holmes, a senior sales manager, immediately spoke up. "Gwen, you've already mentioned the fact about low sales and morale," he said. "But we all feel stuck. We're in a rut. We keep doing the same thing while expecting different results. And that, as we now know, is the definition of insanity."

"Yeah," Mark Rand, the newest manager on the team, chimed in, "we have people who are poorly trained. They might have OK sales skills, but their knowledge of the drugs they're selling is really lacking. The docs just don't pay attention to them."

"And we don't act as a unit," added Lindsay Keating, sales star-extraordinaire. "Everyone is a bit paranoid about helping anybody else. It seems that if we help someone, they do better and then we are rated lower. That's a terrible way to do business. We need to start measuring and encouraging more of what we want."

"OK. So the Present Story looks kind of bleak," said Gwen. "And it seems to me we've put way too much emphasis on these problems in the past six to twelve months. Thank goodness it doesn't have to stay that way, right?" All across the room heads nodded in agreement.

"So let's start with this question: Why does the sales team at ABP exist? What is it we want to do?"

"I know for me, one of the reasons I wanted to get into the pharmaceutical business was to help people," said Alice Francon, a newly promoted sales manager. "I knew I was never going to be a doctor or a nurse, but I like people and I'm good at selling things. So I thought if I could get doctors and nurses what they needed, the medications, then I'd be a part of helping people get well. I think what's most important for me is I want to work for a company that makes a product that reduces illness and suffering," she concluded.

"I like that idea!" Gwen wrote *lasting benefit = reduces illness/suffering* on the flip chart.

"Anyone else?"

"I think we need to make better use of our staff," said Brad.

"In what way?" asked Gwen.

"Most of us at this level are fairly well educated and experienced. But sometimes when ABP needs to do something, it hires a consultant or partners with another group," Brad explained. "Sometimes we need outside help because fresh eyes never hurt, but other times, I think we overlook the talent we have. Some of our people have the skills to do what we hire outsiders to do. If we had a way of moving people around to meet different needs as they arise, we could do more building from within."

"I disagree a bit," interrupted Carl Cameron, the marketing manager, "I think we do too much on our own. We could do a lot more if we worked with other organizations, like this project with ALMR. We're working on the same things, anyway. I know we have to stay competitive with other drug companies, but they have the stuff that we need to expand.

"I know this isn't really a sales issue, but it kind of goes along with the idea of collaboration," he continued. "I'd like ABP to be a company that's really respected by other health care companies because we have what they need to succeed."

"Can you expand on that?" asked Gwen.

"We're not the biggest dog on the block, so to speak, and we may never reach that point, but what if the big dogs always came to us when they needed new technologies or patents or formulas to make their brands? I guess what I'm thinking is that instead of trying to be the company on top, let's be the company that the company on top can't live without."

"I like the way you think, Carl. These are all really good ideas, but they might be a bit beyond the scope of the sales department. We'll certainly keep them on the list, but what I'd like to do now is focus specifically on our department. Let me ask you this, if all the problems that we listed as part of our Present Story were solved, what would our sales effort look like?"

"First of all, I think we would be more of a team," said Brad. "With sales down, people are afraid that there might be budget cuts and they'll lose their jobs. That creates an environment of looking out for number one. We stop being open and honest with each other. We try to protect our own territory."

"Let's translate that into a clear statement about the future. What does the story say?" Gwen prodded.

"Yes. I want to see us try new things in the sales department," added Lindsay. "We don't have much control over the actual product or the market, but we can change how we approach them. It's like Abby said in her talk yesterday: We can't always control what happens, but we can control our attitude and our response."

"So, more innovation in how we get the word out about our products?" Gwen clarified as she wrote *sales innovation* on the chart. "That's really what Challenge the Process is all about."

"That works for me," said Alice. "I'm kind of passionate about change, and to tell you the truth, I'm feeling pretty restless right now because we just do the same old thing every year. There's no new sales ideas or really any incentives for having them."

"Yeah," agreed Carl. "Abby and Sam have been telling us about these pyromaniac companies that burn their policy manuals and celebrate stuff all the time. I don't think we celebrate much. We should celebrate people and new ideas more."

"And maybe, if we were more innovative and we were more open and honest, we'd attract better people," added Carl. "Not that there's anything wrong with who we have now," he added quickly. "It's just that sometimes we only focus on the sales and the dollars and forget that we make a difference. All of us should be motivated to make a difference and we should only hire new people who share that vision."

"I think that would change our entire focus," said Gwen excitedly. "If sales was about making a difference in people's lives, and not about how many dollars we brought in, that would certainly change our attitude and our mood. You hear that, Jerry?" she shouted to the back of the room where Jerry, Abby, and Sam were seated. "We're busting out of our rut!" The room laughed. *God, that felt good,* thought Gwen.

"I'm all for it," said Jerry. "You write the future story and together we'll make it happen."

"You heard the boss—I mean our leader!" Gwen beamed, and added, "Let's give him something that knocks his socks off. Let's take a look at what we've got here. According to our ideas, here on the flip chart ABP is a great company because—

"It develops products that provide lasting benefits and alleviates significant human suffering.

"It collaborates with others *and* builds from within to build a flexible yet enduring organization.

"It delivers drug technologies that power the most success-ful brands in the industry.

"It fosters an open and honest employee environment.

"It celebrates innovation.

"It attracts bright, motivated employees who want to make a difference.

"How do you feel about all that?" Gwen asked, holding her breath. *Will they take the bait?* For a moment, there was nothing but wide-eyed silence and then, from the back of the room, Sam began to applaud. Soon the entire room was whistling and cheering. As she exhaled, Gwen felt the tension leave her body.

"OK, team! Let's pull it back together for a minute," she shouted over the celebration. "We're not done yet!" She grabbed a red marker and wrote *"Making a difference in people's lives!"* across the top of a new sheet of paper. "It sounds like we've touched on our passion," she said, pointing to the words. "Now we need to start breaking these six big ideas into the chunks that Sam and Abby talked about. Obviously, we won't be able to nail down everything this afternoon, but let's take a giant leap toward it." With a renewed enthusiasm welling up in the room, Gwen forged ahead with the Never-Ending Story process.

As the groups plunged into their assignment, Gwen eased her way to the back of the room and collapsed into the seat beside Jerry.

"You did it, kid," he grinned, giving her shoulder a squeeze.

"We'll see," said Gwen. "We'll see."

CHAPTER 19

Embrace the Struggle
Wednesday—5:17 PM

Gordon gazed around the lobby, drumming his fingers on the arm of his chair. The whole situation with Joe's apparent attitude change makes this meeting with Gwen Kelly a bit sticky, he thought. Still, he wasn't completely sold on Joe's epiphany. The guy's pulled the wool over a lot of people's eyes in the past, thought Gordon. He wasn't interested in being the next fool on Joe's list. The sight of Gwen striding through the front door caught his eye. *Here goes.*

"Gwen! Hello!" He rose and thrust out his hand.

"Hello Gordon, it's nice to see you again." *Be confident, Gwen,* she said to herself, taking a deep breath. You want this one. She'd spent the better part of the time between her last session and this meeting at the spa, and a quick pick-me-up pedicure had calmed her nerves, for the most part.

"You too," replied Gordon. "I don't know if you're surprised by this turn of events, but I have to admit I was."

"It does seem serendipitous," admitted Gwen.

"I've reserved a small conference room for about an hour," said Gordon. "Shall we?" He led her back toward the meeting rooms.

When they had settled into their seats, Gordon pulled a sheaf of papers from his folder. "Typically ALMR goes through a more formal process with an interview panel and the like, but since we're both here at the same place, let's view this time as sort of a pre-interview phase. I want to get a sense of who you are as a person and as a leader, and I'd like to share some of my vision for the company to see if it aligns with your values. Does that work for you?"

Gwen pulled a notepad from her purse. "Yes, sir."

"Great. Then let's start by having you tell me what you're doing now and why you're looking for a change."

Gwen took a deep breath. "I've been sales director at Advanced Biomolecular Pharmaceuticals for two years. But I've been in the Sales Department for seven years. Before that, I was the senior sales associate at G&G. I didn't start out with the intention of working in the pharmaceutical business—I actually wanted to be an advertising executive, but over time, I've come to really care about the industry. I like the idea of creating a product that makes a difference in people's lives. One of my daughters, Lisa, has asthma—so I've seen firsthand how the research that goes on behind the scenes eventually touches the public in a very profound way."

"What attracted you to the sales arena?" asked Gordon.

"The flexibility, really," said Gwen. "I like getting out of the office and meeting people, and it was an easier position to work around my family."

"And management? How do you enjoy the challenge of leading a team?"

Gwen paused. How was she going to answer that one? Honestly? Who'd hire someone who claimed to struggle with leadership? "I'm a great manager. I love structure and organization, charts and tables, mapping it all out on paper. As you're certainly aware, the market's been in a bit of a slump so sales are down across the board, but I expect our numbers to pick up again when our new products hit the market in the next quarter."

"It sounds like you're fairly comfortable where you're at," noted Gordon. "Why does the vice president of sales position at ALMR pique your interest?"

"Upward mobility, primarily. I feel a bit like I'm stuck in one spot right now. I'd like a new set of challenges."

Gordon jotted a few notes on the page in front of him. "What types of opportunities do you anticipate at ALMR?"

"Different people, for one thing," said Gwen. "A new climate, different products, more responsibility, that sort of thing. I'm ready for that challenge."

Gordon leaned back in his seat and folded his hands behind his head. "Gwen, this isn't a formal interview, so I'm going to step out of my 'interviewer' role here for a second and be candid with you. I asked our HR person to talk to Jerry Allen, your manager, about you. He had nothing but good things to say about your work. In fact, he said you're an outstanding employee in every area except one. Leadership. And I've noticed you've already sidestepped the issue in our conversation here."

Gwen's heart sank.

"Abby Bancroft has been my leadership coach for a few years now," continued Gordon, "and you've just sat through two days of her workshops, so you can imagine the type of leader I'm looking for to fill this position. Do you think you're that person?"

"Uh, I'm not sure. I've actually had a lot of time to think about that over the past two days, and I honestly don't know." Gwen sighed. There. The truth was out. *Take it or leave it, Gordon,* she thought. *It's your call.*

"I know you're not aware of this, Gwen, but after I found out yesterday you were the candidate that Jodi Eastridge recommended, I listened in on your afternoon session today," said Gordon.

"I didn't know," Gwen said, startled.

"I was impressed."

"Really?"

"Absolutely," said Gordon. "It's obvious to me you're capable of using The Five Practices when you want to. What I want to know is why you don't do those things all the time?"

Gwen felt the familiar pull of fear in her chest. *What am I afraid of?* she wondered. She ran her fingers through her hair and rested her chin in her palm, gazing toward the long bank of windows. Everything looked so peaceful here, with the sunset and the mountains. Nothing like home, where her job and her family demanded so much of her. If only there was a way to balance the two. *Balance.* That was the word she'd chosen as her core value and yet it seemed like such an elusive concept. *But that's it,* she thought. *That's what's holding me back.*

"Gwen?" Gordon leaned forward and smiled at her. "What's on your mind? Step out of the interview for a minute here and let's just talk about leadership."

"I'm worried about my family," she said. "Do you have kids, Gordon?"

"Two boys," he smiled at the thought of Terry and Brent. "Both grown, college students."

"Then maybe you'll understand," Gwen said. "There's only so much of me to go around. I'm a great manager, but a leader, well, that's a whole other realm, and I just don't know if I can commit the time to it. I already work so hard. I put in so many hours and spend so much time away from my husband and my girls, that, frankly, I'm miserable. If I become a great leader too, how much more time away from my family would that take?"

"Leadership *is* a commitment, Gwen," Gordon said, "but as intelligent as you are, I don't think you fully grasp how it works. I get the impression that you view leadership as one more thing to add to your already lengthy to-do list. But it doesn't work that way. Leadership isn't a structure that you superimpose on top of your life in progress. It's a complete way of life in and of itself.

"Do you understand?"

"Evidently not."

"Look, you've said yourself you're miserable in your current job," Gordon prompted. "What makes you think you'll be any happier at ALMR?"

"It's like I said earlier," explained Gwen. "I'd be working with different people and products, and I'd have more responsibility."

"But most likely you'd also have the same problems," Gordon pointed out. "People are generally the same anywhere you go, Gwen, and if you're unhappy with yourself, it won't matter whether you're selling drug technology or used cars, you're still going to be unhappy."

"Then what *is* the solution?" asked Gwen in frustration. "Because believe me, I'm willing to try anything at this point."

"I think you're willing to do anything except embrace the struggle you're in," said Gordon. "The struggle is part of the success, Gwen."

"I just don't see it that way, I guess."

"Gwen, I'm a country boy, and I loved exploring the land around our home. One day, when I was just a kid, I found a cocoon dangling from a small tree limb. I was going to cut it down and put it in a jar so I could watch it hatch, but then I decided to go back and check on it every day instead. I did this for a few days and nothing happened. But one day, I noticed a small hole at the top of the cocoon and I was so excited because I could see the future butterfly wiggling around a bit inside. I tried to be patient to wait for the bug to emerge on its own, but curiosity got the better of me and I thought I would help him get out, so I used my pocketknife to cut a bigger hole. It seemed to be working because the butterfly moved around even more. So I got more excited and cut the cocoon all the way open. I couldn't wait to see him spread his wings and fly. But then the saddest thing happened. The butterfly flopped out of the cocoon onto the dirt below and as it struggled to open its wings, it just gave up and died. Do you know why?"

"Not really," said Gwen.

"It turns out that the struggle to emerge from the cocoon is actually part of the growth process for butterflies," Gordon explained. "If they don't push against the boundaries of their casing, their wings don't develop the strength they need to fly. I see you in that position right now, Gwen. You've got a struggle on your hands at ABP, but you may not become the leader you're supposed to be unless you go through it. You've got to deal with yourself first, Gwen. Leadership is who you are before it's something that you do. Real leadership creates balance. You need to get off the fence. I don't make promises lightly," said Gordon, "but I promise you if you make the choice from manager to leader, you'll be more fulfilled professionally and personally. When you're happy at home, you'll be a better employee. When you're successful at work, your husband and kids will be able to see the difference at home. That's the balance that everyone is longing to achieve."

"It's a nice idea, but—"

"It's more than an idea, Gwen, I've been where you are. I only connected with Abby a few years ago," said Gordon. "Before that, I was just like you, trying to keep all the balls in the air, talking the talk but not walking the walk. However, my passion was missing in action at work and at home. Once I made the choice, my workmates and my family had a new role model. They gladly joined up. When you put your heart into what you're doing, you're going to be successful whether you work for ALMR or you stay at ABP."

"Does that mean you're not interested in interviewing me further?" asked Gwen.

"Of course not," smiled Gordon. "You'd be a real asset to our team. But my concern is you're running away from something you don't want rather than running toward something you really care about."

162 | THE OFFSITE

"So what now?" asked Gwen. "I mean, you pretty much know all about my weaknesses here. Doesn't that put me at a disadvantage with other candidates?"

"Not necessarily. You're a high-quality candidate, Gwen. We'd be lucky to get you. But you need to spend more time thinking about what you really want. Who you really want to be."

"OK . . ."

"As far as I'm concerned, the door's still open. Why don't you take a few days to think about it, and if you're still interested in coming to work at ALMR, I want it to be because you're clear about your passion. You can call me directly then and we'll set up a formal interview in San Diego."

Gwen accepted the business card Gordon slid across the table. "Thank you," she said. "You've given me a lot to think about."

"That's what leaders do, Gwen. They ask the questions that need asking."

CHAPTER 20

What's Real Matters!

Thursday—8:29 AM

Gwen sipped her coffee and gazed out over the pool. She'd decided to forgo the group breakfast to spend a few minutes alone. Awake most of the night, she'd thought about Gordon's words. "My concern is you're running away from something you don't want, rather than running toward something you really care about." *He's right*, thought Gwen, drinking in the morning air. *I've been running for years. Maybe that's why I'm so tired.*

"Gwen?" Sam sat down on a chair beside her. Deep in thought, she hadn't even heard him approach.

"Good morning, Sam. How are you?"

"I think by now you know the answer to that one," chuckled Sam.

"Perfect, right?"

"You don't look so perfect, though," said Sam. "Is there something on your mind?"

"I'm just going through everything you and Charlie and Abby have said these past few days, trying to figure out how it's all going to work out for me." Gwen rested her chin on her hand and stared intently at Sam. "I had an informal interview with Gordon Murphy last night for the vice president of sales position with ALMR. But then I've also had a chance to get to know Jerry better, and I think I understand what he wants from me now. I'm just not sure if he really sees me as a part of the ABP future. I'm just not sure what do to."

"Have you talked to Jerry about this?" Sam asked.

"I told him about the interview, if that's what you mean, but I haven't talked to him since last night when I met with Gordon," replied Gwen.

"I don't think Jerry's plans are as mysterious as you might imagine. You know I've been watching you this week, Gwen— you're like a sponge, soaking up all this leadership stuff. My gut tells me Jerry sees that too. No one can make this decision for you, but if you want my opinion, you need to stop worrying about what other people expect of you and ask yourself what you expect from yourself."

"But how do I know what that is?" asked Gwen.

"When you were sitting in Abby's keynote address, did you pick out some core values?"

"Yes."

"Do you remember what they were?" Sam asked.

"My number one was *balance* . . . and I think the others were *family, health, excellence,* and *spirituality.*"

"Those are great choices, Gwen. From what little I know of you, they seem like a good fit." Sam could see the struggle in her eyes. "I think the next step for you is to decide which opportunity helps you connect most with those values. And I think you should talk to Jerry."

"Thanks, Sam. I'll keep that in mind." Gwen had reached the dregs of her coffee. "Do you have the time?"

"Ten to nine."

"Seriously?" Gwen sprang to her feet. "I'm addressing our team in ten minutes. Shoot! I've got to run. Thanks for everything, Sam!" Gwen grabbed her purse and headed for the Tucson Ballroom.

Jerry paced back and forth near the podium. He hadn't checked in with Gwen after her interview last night. He had no idea what state of mind she'd be in. "What was I thinking, asking her to do the main closing event when she's got one foot out the door?" he muttered. When she'd told him about the interview with ALMR, it had really thrown him. He knew she was struggling, but he'd had no idea it'd gone this far. One of his primary goals for this whole offsite had been to coax Gwen into leadership. And now that she was almost there, she was thinking about jumping ship.

Gwen strode quickly across the ballroom. "I'm so sorry for running a bit late. I took my coffee by the pool and ended up talking to Sam."

Sam, huh. Well maybe that was a good sign. Sam would point her in the right direction. The question was, what would that direction be. "Are you ready?" Jerry asked.

There's no point in trying to hide it, she thought. "To be honest, I've never been less sure of myself than I am at this moment."

"And that's supposed to reassure me?" said Jerry with a nervous laugh.

"Is it working?" Gwen asked.

"Not one iota," Jerry replied. "Before you go up there, Gwen, I just want you to know, whatever decision you eventually make about your career, I believe in you. But that will never be enough if you don't believe in yourself."

"Thanks Jerry, you've always supported me, and for that, I'm truly grateful."

Jerry reached out and put his hand on her arm. "All right, Gwen, knock 'em dead."

"Good morning, everyone," said Gwen to the assembled ABP sales team. "Because this is our last session together before we head home, I wanted to take a few minutes to thank the team that has worked so hard to make these past few days an engaging and informative experience. First of all, a round of thanks goes out to Abby Bancroft and the team from Perfect Leadership Consulting. You've given us a lot to think about, and for that we are truly grateful." The room erupted with applause. "And of course our own Patty who coordinated everything on our end.

"I also want to thank Mary Mitchell, the assistant manager of La Mariposa, and the entire team of hotel employees who have made this a flawless event," said Gwen.

"They've gone to great lengths to serve you during the week and they've done a spectacular job of doing so. If you agree, please stand and join me in applauding them."

The outpouring of respect and gratitude overwhelmed the hotel staff lined up across the front of the room. Gwen could see them standing a little taller, a few wiping tears from their eyes.

It had been Abby who'd asked her to say thank you to the staff. *I'm not sure I would have done that on my own,* she thought. *And yet, what a difference it makes.* Gwen turned her attention back to the audience.

"I did have a long speech to share with you today. I had plenty of data points on a whole bunch of PowerPoint slides, the works." She could almost hear them groan. "The key word is *did,*" she said with a smile. "But I've learned something from our facilitators this week, and so instead I'd like to spend a few minutes sharing from my heart. Someone once said that a leader knows the way, goes the way, and shows the way. And so this morning, I want to illustrate that behavior and let you know about a decision I've made."

"Here it comes," thought Jerry, leaning against the back wall. A hush fell over the room.

"Much of what we heard this week challenged our choices," continued Gwen. "We asked you to think about what you do, and the when, why, and how of doing it. As your teammates, the leadership of ABP has done the same. As I was reflecting on my vision for the team earlier this week, I was heavily influenced by the incredible beauty of the mountains behind this hotel. It dawned on me they were an apt metaphor for our sales team. We are poised to climb. And as Abby pointed out, the only limitations that we have are those we place on ourselves." As the words left Gwen's mouth, they resonated in her heart. She paused. *That's it, Gwen. Your only limitation is you.*

"When we change our beliefs from negative to positive, it's as if a giant weight is lifted from our shoulders." She took a deep breath and felt the weight of the world slip away. It wasn't going to be easy, she knew, but that didn't matter anymore. Gazing at the crowd, Gwen saw each person as if for the first time. Not as a sales team that had let her down, but as a group of people in need of a leader. *They need you, Gwen. Step up to the plate.*

"Things aren't going well in our department," she paused to let the statement register, "and we can blame others all we want, but in this life, we will always have a choice. And I choose to say the days of pointing our fingers elsewhere are over. We have only ourselves, and our negative thoughts and perceptions, to blame. Starting with me."

This wasn't at all what Jerry had been expecting. "Where's she going with this?" he murmured to Sam, who had joined him in the back of the room.

"Since the day I started as sales director at ABP, I've been running from leadership, running from fear," said Gwen. "But leaders don't run from fear. When they experience fear, they do what they have to do, not what's easy to do. Leadership takes courage . . . and at the beginning of this week, I was convinced I did not have the internal power to continue as your leader. I came to this offsite hoping I would find some type of magical formula that would make leadership easier for me. And if I didn't, I would leave the company and start over somewhere else." A buzz rippled through the room. *That certainly got their attention,* thought Gwen.

"Through the sessions this week I realized the problem wasn't the job, or the team—it was me. I haven't been using The Five Practices. I haven't been creating the life that I want to live and I need to acknowledge and accept the power I possess to change. As I said earlier, our sales team is poised to climb. After the past two days, some of you are probably already at the base camp preparing your assault on the summit. You have the supplies and the tools you need to begin your journey. The only thing missing for your climb is a competent, courageous leader." There was no backing down now. She scanned the room, trying to look each person in the eye until she settled on Jerry and Sam.

"I would like to be that person," said Gwen. "I want to help you find your passion, your courage, and your success. I want you to join me in our quest. I want us to stand on that peak, together." In that moment of surrender, Gwen realized for the first time she was truly happy.

Jerry breathed a sigh of relief. *She did it!*

"I've found my passion," said Gwen, a grin spreading across her face. "It's helping our customers live better, healthier lives. Lives where illness doesn't take them away from their families, their careers, and their passions. We don't sell pharmaceuticals or drug technology, we give hope. We give nobodies back the feeling of being somebody. I am making a renewed commitment to you, and I am asking you to do the same to me." She reached into her folder. "I want to read you this quote from Karen Raun. 'Only as high as we reach can we grow. Only as far as we seek can we go. Only as deep as we look can we see. Only as much as we dream can we be.' Under my leadership, I want to take you higher and deeper than we've ever been before. Our work matters . . . because we matter . . . because each and every one of you matters."

Gwen stepped back from the podium, her heart pounding. One by one, people began to rise, applause filling the room.

Sam leaned over to Jerry. "I think we have another leader for the revolution."

"I think you're right, Sam," Jerry said as the two of them slipped quietly out the back door.

PART FOUR

Separate Ways

CHAPTER 21

Success Is Assured
Thursday—12:24 PM

"So, how did you think it went, Abby?" Sam asked as he munched at his club sandwich. They'd agreed to meet for lunch before Abby left for home.

"Perfect," replied Abby with a grin. "I don't think I could have planned it better myself. Thank you again for agreeing to speak to the group and for spending so much time with Gwen's team. I really should put you on the PLC payroll, you know."

"Unnecessary," said Sam. "It's a worthy investment. I've always known you were worth the time, Abby. I don't invest my time, or my money, in just anything. Your ROI has been a joy to watch, just like my investment in this hotel. It's all in the passion."

"What do you mean your investment in the hotel?" quizzed Abby. "You mean the time you spend gardening here?"

"Yes, and the money."

"What money?"

"Well I am the local principal investor in this hotel—and the managing partner," said Sam with a wink. "But let's keep that between us. If most of the staff knew, they'd never let me get away with playing gardener, and I need my fun."

"You never cease to amaze me, Sam," laughed Abby.

"Or you me. You know when I interviewed Mary Mitchell for the assistant manager position, she mentioned you as someone who had had a significant impact on her life. She obviously didn't know we're friends, but as soon as I knew you had led her into leadership, as indirect as it might have been at the time, I knew she would be the real deal. She's got a lot of leadership potential. It won't be too long before she's running the whole place."

"So does that mean you'll be retiring yet again?" quipped Abby.

"You know retirement's not really for me," said Sam. "My work here allows me to stay relaxed. I do have a quiet office onsite where I can focus on my writing and lecturing. I also keep all my investments growing . . . if you know what I mean."

"You're going to outlive us all, Sam. You'll be a wizened old man, hobbling around this place still leaving a legacy after the rest of us have faded from sight."

"I have total confidence in you, Abby," replied Sam. "I can't even imagine a future for you that doesn't include success."

Gordon, Gwen, and Jerry sat at a small table in the Clubhouse Deli. "Now that Gwen's definitely made her decision to stay with ABP, let me apologize for any awkwardness our interview might have caused this week," said Gordon. "It really was a blind interview set up by a recruiter."

"Not a problem," replied Jerry. "I'm just glad that you've found your place, Gwen. If you had gone over to ALMR, you would have left some big shoes to fill, but we would have still had the chance to work together through the partnership."

"What are you going to do about the position?" asked Gwen. "I understand that the man who previously held it—Joe, was that his name?—is stepping down?"

"Joe is actually going to be moving back into business development," said Gordon. "It's a big step for him. I thought we were going to have to let him go, but he seems to be serious about making some changes. We'll see. It's really more than we could have hoped for, but it does leave that VP position open—and since Gwen was our top lead, we're still in the market, I guess. If you know of anyone, Jerry, send them my way."

Jerry waved down their waitress. "Can we get the check, please?"

"It's been taken care of, sir," said the woman with a sly smile.

"By whom?" asked Gordon.

"Someone who wants to make sure your stay at La Mariposa was perfect."

CHAPTER 22

The Perfect Choice
Thursday–3:46 PM
(Tucson Airport)

Abby stared out the concourse window at the planes lining up for takeoff. Exhilarated but exhausted, she leaned her head back against her seat. The teams had come so far. And Joe, well that was damn near a miracle. It was what she loved best about her job, the ability to help others discover they had choices. And that each choice was a creative act. She couldn't wait to hear from Gordon on how Joe progressed in his new role.

And speaking of choices. What was she going to do about Charlie? What could she do? She had her life, her career, and, when she stopped to consider it, Dennis back home. Dennis, who was always there for her even when she sometimes wished he wouldn't be. Dennis, so kind and loving and predictable, and, well, boring if she was perfectly honest. But he loved her, and Abby supposed, in her way, she loved him too. But was that enough? Dennis would be waiting at baggage claim with flowers and that lost puppy look that at first she had found so endearing, but now only seemed to irritate her. It wasn't his fault he no longer sparked a passion in her . . . not like Charlie.

Abby reached into her bag and pulled out the copy of *Bride* magazine she'd picked up at a kiosk after getting her boarding pass. Thumbing through the magazine, she tried to picture herself in one of the sleek white gowns. "This is wrong," she whispered. "I shouldn't be gown shopping unless I'm really going to say yes." She removed the velvet case from her purse and slipped the diamond ring onto her left hand just as the P.A. system crackled to life. She studied it, stretching out her hand so the diamonds sparkled in the overhead lighting.

"This is the final call for Delta Airlines flight 3960 to New York City's JFK airport, now boarding through gate 14."

Her heart began to pound. New York. Charlie. Home. Dennis. The words ran round and round in her head. She glanced from gate 14 back to her glittering finger before slipping the ring back into its box.

Make the choice. Just say yes. . . .

Thursday—5:49 PM
(New York City)

Charlie was in his quiet zone in the Waldorf's Speaker Preparation Room. He'd had a hard time getting the Tucson offsite out of his mind. As soon as business was wrapped on Wednesday, he'd caught the last flight to New York. He'd thought waking up in a new city would help him clear his head, but after a long jog and a hot shower, he was still thinking about Abby. And sleep, forget about it. Every time he closed his eyes, he saw her face.

That scene by the pool had almost completely derailed him. He should have talked to her, apologized, at least left things on better terms from a work standpoint. He'd tried to call her several times on Wednesday night from the airport but she didn't answer. He'd left a message on her answering machine and then called back twice more just to hear her voice. *You're an idiot, Charlie. You're an idiot if you think a relationship like that is just going to breeze through your life again.*

He took a deep breath and bounced up and down on the balls of his feet, getting into game mode. As he headed up the stairs into the waiting auditorium, his cell phone rang to life.

"Do you want me to answer it, sir?" the assistant called after him.

"I'm in the zone, Cliff," Charlie hollered over his shoulder. "Let it go to voice mail."

The Beginning

The Five Practices and Ten Commitments of Leadership

Practice	Commitment
Model the Way	1. Clarify values by finding your voice and affirming shared ideals. 2. Set the example by aligning actions with shared values.
Inspire a Shared Vision	3. Envision the future by imagining exciting and ennobling possibilities. 4. Enlist others in a common vision by appealing to shared aspirations.
Challenge the Process	5. Search for opportunities by seizing the initiative and by looking outward for innovative ways to improve. 6. Experiment and take risks by constantly generating small wins and learning from experience.
Enable Others to Act	7. Foster collaboration by building trust and facilitating relationships. 8. Strengthen others by increasing self-determination and developing competence.
Encourage the Heart	9. Recognize contributions by showing appreciation for individual excellence. 10. Celebrate the values and victories by creating a spirit of community.

Source: The Leadership Challenge, Fourth Edition, by James M. Kouzes and Barry Z. Posner. Copyright 2007 John Wiley & Sons, Inc. Used with permission.

Acknowledgments (Gratitude)

Leadership is a choice about creating open, honest, and authentic relationships that urge others to want to discover their power and focus on what matters to them and their community. With that in mind, this book is dedicated to all who have pushed, pulled, and "provoked" me through my life journey (so far). To you I offer my abundant gratitude. Together we have overcome obstacles or reframed them into opportunities. We've learned from each other. The revolution continues. Our masterpiece awaits. So, Onward!

As Sam made clear earlier, the specific, personal thank-you note is the best way to offer appreciation. Well, please consider this book a huge thank-you note. And now for the specifics:

Jim Kouzes and Barry Posner: You, once again, allow my work to intertwine with yours. I am honored as always. Thank you for the foundation.

Steve Farber: You are a great ally and true sounding board. Your "pay it forward" friendship is deeply appreciated and your coaching instrumental.

Terry Pearce, Tom Peters, and the late Gordon Mackenzie: Your works were an inspiration to me as well as those I am honored to touch.

Allison Shaw: My dialogue "coach." From early structure to content and flow, your talent was essential and our collaboration was the secret ingredient.

To my agents, Jon Malysiak and Scott Adlington: Thanks for showing up at just the perfect time.

To the crew at Jossey Bass: Neal Maillett and Lisa Shannon, your response to the book was more than gratifying and deeply humbling. Thanks for your critical eye. Your choice was perfect! Mary Garrett and Hilary Powers, your eye for detail was the final necessary touch.

To my former Tom Peters Company colleagues and the numerous other leadership gurus I had the opportunity to travel the trails with: This story is our story. Thank you for letting me share the stage with you. Our work together allowed me to Show Up, Speak Up, Step Up, and Serve Up™. Cheers!

To my clients who became friends and my friends who became clients: You allowed me to refine my messages over the years while working with some great people from a variety of walks of life. Our time together allowed hundreds of "thought grenades" to shock everyone's system.

To my former Alza folks, wherever you are: You were the best client (almost family) experience in my speaking career. With special thanks to Dan Swisher, Jay Shepard, John Taylor, and Linda Morrisey. Our work together was perfect. Our time was real. We were all agents of choice. Thank you for allowing me to be "not just a vendor."

And of course to my children: Jeff, Trevor, Rochelle, and Jessica, your love and support through the years, in the midst of my seemingly constant travel, turmoil, and change, has made my life story richer. Thanks for your lessons and learning a few things from "Recycle Man" along the way.

And finally to my wife, Roxane: Our twenty-five-year Sunday kind of love odyssey has been an E-ticket ride through a sometimes Mr. Toad wilderness. You are an amazing believer. A true leader. Your exuberance for life is an inspiration. What's Next?

I'm Loving You All!

The Author

Passion is the driving force behind Robert Thompson's success. As a sought-after speaker, workshop leader, and executive coach, he demonstrates a passion for personal and professional leadership that touches the lives of thousands of people every year. Known for his practical, street-savvy style, Robert offers a fusion of real-life stories and conversational techniques that connects with his audience at an intimate, intense, and individual level. His refreshing approach to leadership is both thoughtful and thought-provoking, engaging participants in open, honest, and authentic interaction. When Robert steps up to the plate, plan to participate and prepare to be challenged.

Robert's thirty years of innovative business experience include a distinguished group of clients—among them Alza, Amgen, AT&T, California State University, Hewlett-Packard, Herman Miller/SQA, Interwoven, Johnson & Johnson, Lawrence Livermore Labs, various local, state, and federal government agencies, Lockheed Martin, Qwest, Seagate, SGI, Sony, Sun Microsystems, The Gap, Trane, the University of California, and Visa. He is the founder of Applied Performance, a leadership and personal communication services company that works with employees on their first jobs, chief executive officers, and every level between. Through the Tom Peters Company, Robert facilitated a number of corporate workshops including the highly acclaimed "The Leadership Challenge." He continues to be a founding Master Facilitator for that program.

Robert created, managed, and sold for profit both a regional newspaper publishing company and a national advertising sales company, which he had guided to international prominence through relationships with Procter & Gamble, General Motors, Bayer, and other high-profile companies. As the founder of a corporate nonprofit exchange program for aspiring post-communist business professionals, Robert attained a key role in the Clinton-Yeltsin "Business for Russia" initiative. Robert served on the board of advisers for a successful Internet start-up company and assisted the group through their initial public offering.

Robert is a graduate of San Jose State University with a degree in journalism, and his thirteen years of experience with the *San Jose Mercury News* has honed his ability to take the pulse of any issue. His passion and commitment to leadership extend beyond his career and touch his community, where he has held an active role in foundation boards, community panels, and a variety of civic commissions. Robert has created or conducted original leadership programs including "Lifetime Leadership," "Sharpening Our Focus," "Ethics in the Workplace," "Lifescapes," and "The Road to Entrepreneurship."

Invite Robert to bring the lessons from *The Offsite* to your next company gathering. For more information or to contact Robert directly, please visit www.leaderinsideout.com or email Robert at rht@earthlink.net or rhtcoach@yahoo.com.